Wales

Wales

BY ANN HEINRICHS

*Enchantment of the World
Second Series*

Children's Press®

A Division of Scholastic Inc.

NEW YORK TORONTO LONDON AUCKLAND SYDNEY
MEXICO CITY NEW DELHI HONG KONG
DANBURY, CONNECTICUT

Frontispiece: Caerphilly Castle

Consultant: John Ellis, Ph.D., Assistant Professor of History, Green Mountain College, Poultney, VT

Please note: All statistics are as up-to-date as possible at the time of publication.

Book production by Herman Adler Design

Library of Congress Cataloging-in-Publication Data

Heinrichs, Ann.
    Wales / by Ann Heinrichs
        p. cm. — (Enchantment of the world. Second series)
        Includes bibliographical references and index.
        ISBN 0-516-22288-0
        1. Wales – Juvenile literature. [1. Wales] I. Title. II. Series.
DA708 .H45 2003
942.9—dc21   2002001643

Acknowledgments

For their kind assistance, the author wishes to thank the staff of the National Trust in Wales and the economic statistics staff of the National Assembly for Wales. She would also like to thank the people of Wales for their unfailing hospitality and warmth.

Cover photo:
View over valley in
Snowdonia, Wales

Contents

CHAPTER

 ONE   The Red Dragon Leads the Way 8

 TWO   Mountains, Valleys, and Coasts 14

 THREE   Wildlife in Wales 26

 FOUR   Princes, Saints, and Struggles 36

 FIVE   Governing the Principality 52

 SIX   Making a Living 64

 SEVEN   Proud to Be Welsh 78

EIGHT   Centuries of Spirituality 88

NINE   Land of Poets and Singers 100

TEN   Everyday Life in Wales 114

Coastal footpath

Timeline.....................**128**

Fast Facts....................**130**

To Find Out More...........**134**

Index........................**136**

Celtic bronze shield

CHAPTER ONE

The Red Dragon Leads the Way

I MAGINE A CHRISTMAS EVE BLANKETED WITH NEW-FALLEN snow drifting high against cottages and trees. Children plunge their mittened hands into the snowdrifts and pack snowballs for some serious mischief. Soon owls are hooting in the crisp moonlight, the wind is whistling through the trees, and it's time to hurry home.

All is cozy inside. Chestnuts are roasting on the crackling fire and the smells of pudding and roast turkey fill the air. The

Opposite: **The sun rises after a snowfall on the hills of Wales.**

Children enjoy holiday festivities.

children open their gifts—an oversized muffler (scarf), a scratchy woolen vest, and a clockwork mouse. After dinner, the children huddle around the fireplace and listen to scary stories. They dare not look over their shoulders—they might see a ghost or a troll! Then jolly aunts and uncles sing hearty Christmas songs until, at last, the children are tucked in their beds.

This Christmas scene is part of a grown-up's tender memories of childhood. It comes from *A Child's Christmas in Wales*, a classic tale by Dylan Thomas, Wales's greatest modern poet.

Thomas lived in southern Wales, where many customs were borrowed from neighboring England. Things were quite different in the north, where most people still spoke Welsh. Their Christmas was drenched in old Welsh traditions. They gathered to sing hymns before dawn, boiled up huge kettles of toffee, and feasted on tasty lamb. Children ran from house to house begging for treats.

In spite of these regional differences, though, all Welsh people share many traditions. Wales is called the land of poets. Fifteen centuries ago, Welsh poets were honored storytellers who passed on heroic tales through their poems. That tradition survives today in Wales's *eisteddfod*—a cultural festival in which the finest poet takes the highest prize. Wales is also called the land of song. Singing in choirs is another centuries-old tradition that's still practiced today.

Wales is a land of myth, magic, and legend—of giants, fairies, princes, and saints. Stone monuments, crosses, and castles stand across the countryside as reminders of the misty past. Even the land itself is steeped in folklore. A mountain

could be a boulder hurled by a giant, and a river might be a dragon's home. And everywhere—from bumper stickers to rugby players' shirts to the national flag—you see the red dragon, an ancient symbol of Wales.

Politically, Wales is part of the United Kingdom of Great Britain and Northern Ireland (Great Britain includes England, Scotland, and Wales)—the UK. This union came about after the Welsh people had fought off invaders for centuries. Yet, all those years, they struggled fiercely to hold on to their Welsh identity. A major battleground in this struggle was the ancient Welsh language.

Geopolitical map of Wales

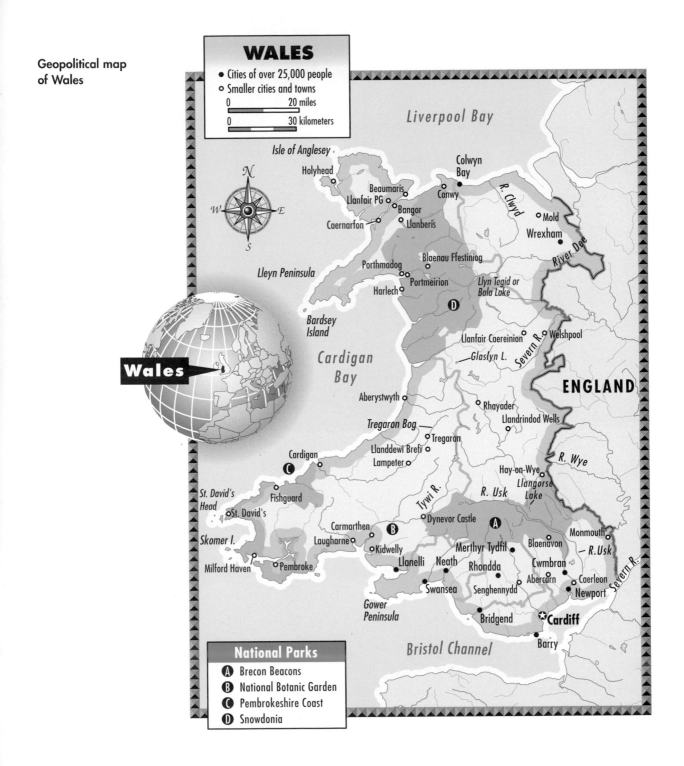

WALES

- ● Cities of over 25,000 people
- ○ Smaller cities and towns

0 — 20 miles
0 — 30 kilometers

Liverpool Bay

Isle of Anglesey

Holyhead

Colwyn Bay

Beaumaris
Llanfair PG
Conwy
Bangor
Llanberis
Caernarfon

R. Clwyd

Mold
Wrexham

River Dee

Blaenau Ffestiniog

Porthmadog
Portmeirion

Lleyn Peninsula

Harlech

Llyn Tegid or Bala Lake

D

Bardsey Island

Wales

Cardigan Bay

Llanfair Caereinion

Welshpool

Severn R.

Glaslyn L.

ENGLAND

Aberystwyth

Rhayader

Llandrindod Wells

Tregaron Bog

Tregaron

Llanddewi Brefi
Lampeter

R. Wye

Cardigan

Hay-on-Wye

Llangorse Lake

C

St. David's Head

Fishguard

St. David's

Skomer I.

Carmarthen

Laugharne

Kidwelly

B

Tywi R.

Dynevor Castle

R. Usk

A

Monmouth

R. Usk

Blaenavon

Merthyr Tydfil

Rhondda

Cwmbran

Abercarn

Caerleon

Milford Haven

Pembroke

Llanelli

Neath

Swansea

Senghennydd

Newport

Gower Peninsula

Bridgend

Severn R.

☆ Cardiff

Barry

Bristol Channel

National Parks

- Ⓐ Brecon Beacons
- Ⓑ National Botanic Garden
- Ⓒ Pembrokeshire Coast
- Ⓓ Snowdonia

Today, Wales is officially bilingual, and Welsh speakers have equal opportunity under the law. Street signs are in Welsh and English, and Welsh is a required subject in the schools. Wales now has its own General Assembly, too—a lawmaking body separate from the UK's Parliament.

Wales looks forward to a future as rich and exciting as its past, guided by a proud motto: "The Red Dragon Leads the Way!"

The red dragon leads the way in this parade.

Mountains, Valleys, and Coasts

"IF WALES WERE ROLLED OUT AS FLAT AS ENGLAND," someone once joked, "it would be the bigger country of the two." That might not be far from the truth! Thousands of years ago, Wales was covered with huge glaciers—sheets of ice. As they moved slowly along, the glaciers dumped boulders and stony gravel across the land. They carved deep valleys and sheared off low peaks, leaving behind plateaus, while Wales's tallest peaks survived. The coastline is rough and rugged, too, with jagged cliffs and many inlets and bays.

Wales is a large peninsula on the west coast of the island of Great Britain. It shares the island with England and Scotland. Wales is actually quite small. It could fit inside the U.S. state of Massachusetts, with room to spare.

Wales is a peninsula, surrounded by water on three sides. Its north coast faces the Irish Sea. Just off Wales's northwest coast is the Isle of Anglesey.

Ireland lies west of Wales, separated from it by Saint George's Channel. Much of the west coast forms an arc around Cardigan Bay, a wide-mouthed

Opposite: **A glacier-carved valley in Nant-yr-Arian near Aberystwyth**

Satellite view of Wales

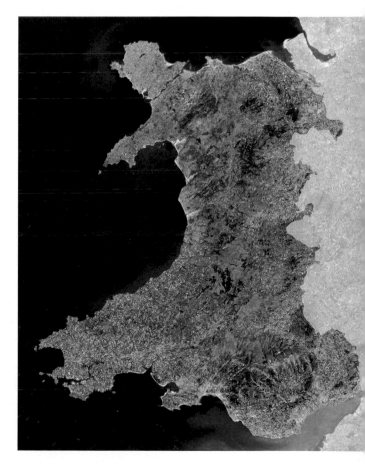

inlet of Saint George's Channel. Two peninsulas reach out into the channel to enclose Cardigan Bay. In the north is Lleyn Peninsula. A large peninsula in the south ends at Saint David's Head. Southern Wales faces the Bristol Channel, an arm of the Atlantic Ocean.

Eastern Wales shares a long border with England. A medieval chieftain named Offa once tried to separate his territory from that of the Welsh tribes by digging a fortified (strengthened) trench along the border. It was called Offa's Dyke. Traces of that trench remain today. This border region is often called the borderlands, or the Borders.

Offa's Dyke passes through the Welsh countryside.

Wales's Geographical Features

Area: 8,015 square miles (20,758 sq km)

Highest Elevation: Mount Snowdon, 3,561 feet (1,085 m) above sea level

Lowest Elevation: Sea level, along the coast

Largest Island: Anglesey, 276 square miles (715 sq km)

Length of Coastline: 614 miles (988 km)

Longest River: Severn River, the longest river in Great Britain, 210 miles (338 km) long

Greatest Distance, North–South: 137 miles (220 km)

Greatest Distance, East–West: 116 miles (187 km)

Shortest Distance, East–West: 40 miles (64 km)

Average January Temperature: 40°F (4.4°C)

Average July Temperature: 61°F (16°C)

Highest Recorded Temperature: 95°F (35°C) at Hawarden Bridge on August 2, 1990

Lowest Recorded Temperature: −10°F (−23.3°C) at Rhayader on January 21, 1940

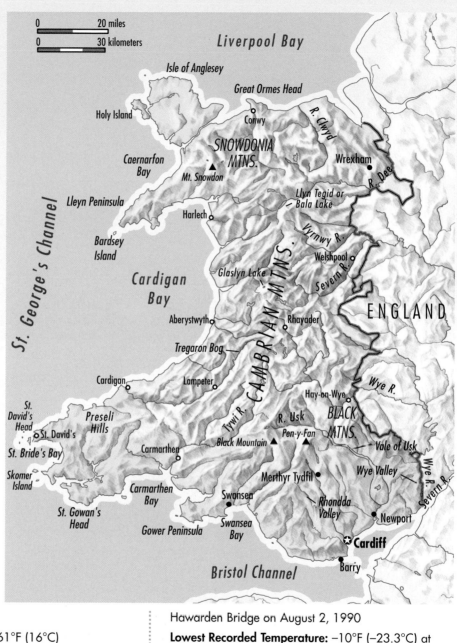

Gently rolling hills of the Cambrian Mountains

Northern Wales

The Cambrian Mountains run from north to south through most of Wales. Their name comes from Cambria, the ancient Roman name for Wales. Because of their very old rocks, the Cambrian Mountains lent their name to the Cambrian geologic period, which took place more than 500 million years ago.

In the north the mountains are rugged and rocky, while those in the south are gently rounded hills. The northern part of the Cambrians is known as the Snowdonia Mountain Range. Much of it is preserved as Snowdonia National Park. High above the park looms Mount Snowdon, Wales's highest peak at 3,561 feet (1,085 meters) above sea level. It's also the second-highest mountain in the UK; only Scotland's Ben Nevis is higher.

Mount Snowdon's Welsh name, *Yr Wyddfa*, means "the tomb." The name recalls a legend that says the mountain is actually an enormous cairn, or pile of stones, erected over the body of a giant slain by King Arthur. Nestled in a valley among Snowdon's crags is Glaslyn Lake. It's tinted green by the copper deposits that lie beneath it. Legend says the lake is green because an *afanc*—a fierce water dragon—lives there.

As mountains go, Snowdon is not very high. It's only about one-eighth the height of Mount Everest, the highest peak in the world (Everest stands on the Nepal-Tibet border). Still, Snowdon's steep, barren slopes give mountain climbers quite a workout. Some members of the British mountain-climbing team that first scaled Everest in 1953 practiced on Snowdon first.

Mount Snowdon

Snowdonia National Park

The Snowdonia National Park region is steeped in history and legend. As a natural fortress, it was the home of the princes of Gwynedd. The ruins of their eleventh-century Dolbadarn Castle still stand.

Although Snowdonia is a national park, it's still open to human settlement. Most of the land is privately owned, and about 27,500 people live and work within the park. It's in the heart of Wales's Welsh-speaking region, and about 65 percent of its residents speak Welsh. Certain areas, however, are protected landscapes, and some of the park's animals and plants are protected species.

Snowdonia National Park extends to the west coast. This stretch of coastline is sometimes called the Cambrian Coast. It runs from the Lleyn Peninsula down to the town of Aberystwyth. Beaches, sand dunes, and high cliffs line the coast, and many castles overlook it. People can explore the coast on railways, along a scenic drive, and on walking paths.

Cambrian Coast beach

Some of Wales's most famous castles are in the north. They include Beaumaris Castle on the island of Anglesey and Conwy and Caernarfon castles in the towns of the same names. The town of Blaenau Ffestiniog used to be the center of northern Wales's slate industry. Portmeirion is a bizarre coastal village built entirely by an eccentric Welsh architect, Sir Clough Williams-Ellis. Its pastel-colored buildings were designed in Italian, Asian, and other styles. The television series *The Prisoner* was filmed in Portmeirion.

Central Wales is much narrower than the north and south. At its narrowest point, Wales is only about 40 miles (64 kilometers) wide. The coastal town of Aberystwyth is the major town in central Wales. Powis Castle, near Welshpool, was a thirteenth-century fortress for the princes of Powys.

View overlooking the fantasy village of Portmeirion

Looking at Wales's Cities

Swansea (below), Wales's second-largest city, has a long history as a shipping port. Today, a renovated, modern Maritime Quarter overlooks its waterfront. Gazing across the Quarter is a statue of poet Dylan Thomas, Swansea's most famous son. The downtown area, bombed during World War II (1939–1945), has been rebuilt, too, but Swansea's old fresh-food market remains. The city's cultural spots include the Swansea Museum and the Guildhall, home of a series of stunning murals. The Dylan Thomas Centre is part of Swansea's National Literature Centre for Wales.

Newport, the third-largest city, grew up as an industrial center in the 1800s. Newport exported coal and iron from its docks at the mouth of the River Usk. The Transporter Bridge is a familiar sight on the Newport skyline. It carries vehicles over the Usk on an aerial gondola. The ruins of Newport Castle remain from medieval times. Even older is the site of Saint Woolos Cathedral on Stow Hill. Early Christians worshiped on this site as far back as the sixth century.

Wrexham is the business center for northeast Wales. The city's Church of Saint Giles dates from the fifteenth century. Its richly ornamented steeple is called one of the Seven Wonders of Wales. Caernarfon, on the Menai Strait, was the port for North Wales's slate industry. It's also home to Caernarfon Castle, a thirteenth-century fortress.

Aberystwyth is the unofficial capital of central Wales. Once the fortress town of King Edward I of England, it sits on the west coast facing Cardigan Bay. Aberystwyth has been a popular seaside resort since the 1800s. Its wide seafront walkway is lined with tall Victorian buildings. Overlooking the town is the University of Wales, founded in 1872. Two century-old railways—the Cliff Railway and the Vale of Rheidol Railway—give visitors scenic views of the countryside.

Monmouth is a historic town on Wales's border with England. Monmouth Castle was the birthplace of Henry V, famous for winning the Battle of Agincourt in 1415. Henry's statue overlooks the town's Agincourt Square. Another statue commemorates Charles Stewart Rolls, cofounder of the Rolls-Royce automobile company. The fortified Monnow Bridge guards the western entry into town.

Southern Wales

Southern Wales is a plateau that's deeply cut by fertile river valleys. This region is often called simply "the Valleys." The Valleys were the heart of Wales's industrial boom in the 1800s. Thousands of miners worked deep underground, digging out rich deposits of coal. Today, Wales's best areas for farming and raising dairy cattle lie in the Valleys. Most of the mines are closed, but mining museums preserve the heritage of the past.

Much of Wales's industry is centered in the south. Southern Wales is the most heavily populated region, too. Clustered around the southern coast are Wales's three largest cities—Cardiff (the capital), Swansea, and Newport. Cardiff sits at the mouth of the Severn, Wales's longest river.

Near Cardiff is the Vale (valley) of Glamorgan, with its charming thatched-roof cottages. The Glamorgan Heritage Coast is a long stretch of beaches, tall dunes, and spectacular

Wales's fertile valleys support farming and grazing.

Dramatic cliffs of the Gower coastline

rocky cliffs. Next to Swansea is the Gower Peninsula, with its dramatic cliffs, beaches, and marshlands. It was the first spot in Great Britain to be declared an Area of Outstanding Natural Beauty. The peninsula has many ancient sites, and smugglers used to hide out in its bays.

Brecon Beacons National Park is in southeast Wales. High, rounded hills as well as forests, lakes, moors, and a network of underground caves lie within the park. The beautiful Wye Valley and the Vale of Usk cuts through the region, too. The Black Mountains lie along the English border on the eastern edge of the park. They are not to be confused with the Black Mountain, a wilderness area in the western part of the park. The Brecon Beacons, however, are the park's central mountain range. Their tallest peak is flat-topped Pen-y-Fan, the highest point in south Wales.

Southwestern Wales is a large peninsula. Its farthest tip is Saint David's Head. This point and the nearby town of Saint David's are named for the patron saint of Wales. He founded a monastery here in the sixth century and is credited with many miraculous deeds. Saint David's Cathedral is a massive stone structure built in the twelfth century. The coastline running along this peninsula is called the Pembrokeshire Coast, another site protected as a national park.

"When elsewhere it is summer, it is winter in Wales." That's how a fourteenth-century Frenchman described Wales's weather. However, Wales is neither colder nor hotter than most parts of the United States. The coldest temperature ever recorded in Wales was only –10° Fahrenheit (–23.3°Celsius), and the highest temperature was 95°F (35°C).

Actually, the sea makes Wales's air warmer in the winter and cooler in the summer. The farther you travel from the sea, the chillier the winters are. In summer, the coast is cooler than inland Wales. So it's possible that the Frenchman was on the coast when he made his summer observations.

Wales is often cloudy due to moist air drifting in from the Atlantic Ocean. The mountainous areas are cloudiest, while the southwestern coastal strip is sunniest. Rainfall also varies widely from one part of Wales to another. Snowdonia and the Brecon Beacons get the most rain, and the wettest months are October through January. Heavy rains in October and November 2000 gave Wales its worst floods in fifty years. Then in December, heavy snows blanketed the countryside. Travel and business came to a halt—but many a Welsh child had a fun-filled Christmas!

A wet, gray day in Snowdonia

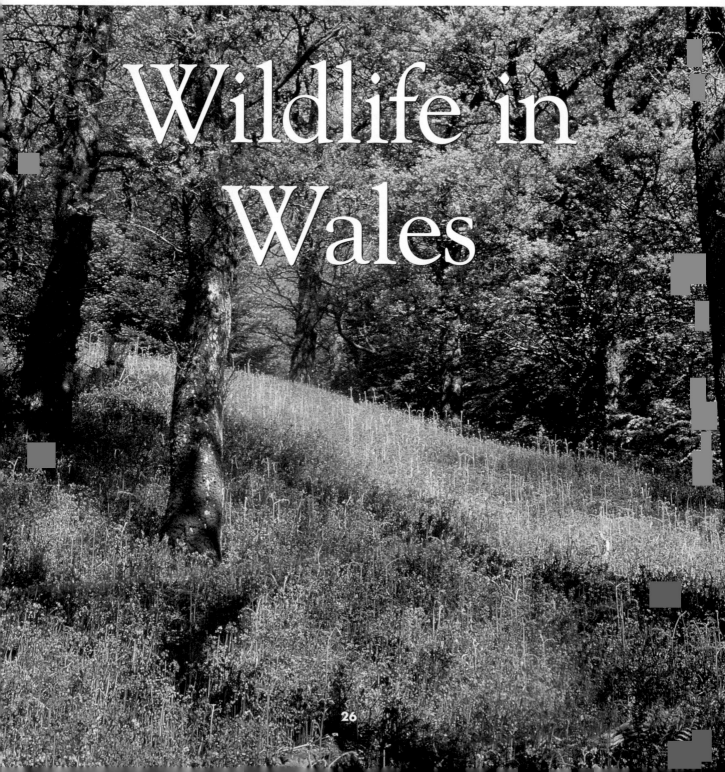

CHAPTER

THREE

Wildlife in Wales

ORESTS ONCE COVERED MUCH OF WALES. OVER TIME, HOW-ever, trees were chopped down to build ships and for fuel, and land was cleared for mining and farming. As the forests disappeared, so did many animals that found shelter there. However, the mountains, river valleys, and shores are still home to an abundance of wildlife. Today, the Welsh government is working hard to preserve these natural habitats.

Opposite: **Protection of the woodlands of Wales is a priority for the Welsh.**

Heather thrives on the moors.

Oak and ash trees line the riverbanks. They provide a shady canopy for wildflowers such as violets, primroses, and wild orchids. Maple and wild cherry trees are common, too.

Wales's moorlands are vast stretches of barren and poorly drained soil. Several tough plants thrive there, though. One is heather—a short, shrubby evergreen with clusters of tiny flowers. Others are bilberry, a type of blueberry, and bog asphodel, an herb of the lily family.

A delicate plant called the Snowdon lily grows only in Snowdonia National Park. Snowdonia also preserves some of Wales's original woodlands of oak, ash, rowan, and hazel trees.

The leek, a rather strong-smelling member of the onion family, has been a Welsh emblem for more than a thousand years.

A woman carries a bundle of newly pulled leeks.

The leek even makes an appearance in William Shakespeare's play *Henry V*. After the Battle of Agincourt, Henry, who was born in the Welsh city of Monmouth, declared, "I wear [the leek] for a memorable honour; For I am Welsh, you know." Traditionally, Welsh people wear leeks in their buttonholes and soldiers wear leeks on their caps on March 1, Saint David's Day.

The leek was once an important part of the Welsh diet. It was also used to cure the common cold, protect against battle wounds and lightning, keep evil spirits away, and foretell the future. Also, if a maiden placed a leek under her pillow, she would see the face of her future husband in her dreams. Today, however, leeks are used in a less romantic fashion—most often in traditional leek and potato soup.

Saint David and the Leek

According to legend, Saint David ordered Welsh soldiers to wear leeks on their helmets when they marched into battle with the Saxons in the A.D. 500s. He said the leeks would help the soldiers to recognize one another in the heat of battle. The Welshmen had a resounding victory, and they were sure that Saint David's leek idea helped them do it. Thus, they cherished the leek as a symbol of their survival. Later, Welsh soldiers wore the leek in 1346 at the Battle of Crécy. Another tradition says that the leek is a symbol of Saint David's simple life. He was a vegetarian, and some say he lived on only water and leeks.

The daffodil is another Welsh symbol associated with Saint David. Daffodils are in bloom around his feast day, and their nickname is "daffy." That's a shortened form of *Dafydd*, the Welsh word for "David."

In modern times people have been wearing daffodils instead of leeks on Saint David's Day. At least, they smell better! Welsh-born British Prime Minister David Lloyd George started the custom. He appeared wearing a daffodil on Saint David's Day and again at an important state ceremony in 1911. Others soon followed his example.

Many Welsh wear daffodils on important occasions.

The National Botanic Garden of Wales

The brand-new National Botanic Garden of Wales just opened in 2000. It spreads across the wooded slopes of the Tywi River Valley in western Wales, once the huge estate of Sir William Paxton. For a century the grounds lay overgrown and neglected. Now, thousands of plant species thrive on the land and in the greenhouses.

Besides being a luxurious recreation area, the garden is a world-class research center. Scientists there study natural habitats such as reed beds, streams, and waterfalls. They also experiment with organic farming, medicinal plants, pollination, and conservation techniques.

The garden's Great Glasshouse is a massive oval greenhouse, sheltering trees and flowers from all over the world. One exhibit honors the memory of the doctors of Myddfai. These medieval country doctors were famous for their herbal-medicine skills.

The National Botanic Gardens' Great Glasshouse

Animals of the Forests and Valleys

Red deer find shelter in Wales's woodlands. Red squirrels leap through the branches and scurry about on the forest floor. Foxes are much bolder than other forest dwellers. They venture out of the woods into farmland and even towns. They've learned to live by raiding garbage cans at night. Feral, or wild, goats can be seen scampering across Snowdonia's high mountainsides. Otters enjoy swimming on their backs in many of Wales's rivers and streams.

Some animals have disappeared from other parts of Great Britain, but in Wales they have managed to hide from civilization—and survive. They include European polecats, pine martens, red kites, and choughs, which are crowlike birds.

The red squirrel is native to Wales's forest.

A polecat ventures out into the bright sunshine.

Polecats roam through Tregaron Bog and other remote areas of north and central Wales. These weasel-like, coarse-coated animals hunt at night. They're sometimes called foul martens because they give off an unpleasant odor when alarmed. The pine marten is another weasel-like forest creature. It's dark brown, with a soft, thick coat.

The White Cattle of Dynevor

The long-horned white cattle of Dynevor are descendants of a truly ancient breed. Druids, the ancient Celtic priests of Wales, valued them as sacrificial animals. When the Romans arrived in Britain, the Druids and their white herds were pushed into Wales, to the island's western fringes.

In medieval times the white cattle were used as payment for debts and fines. Old texts tell of the lords of Dynevor Castle building a good-sized herd from such payments as early as the ninth century A.D. Today the Dynevor cattle now mixed with other breeds, are known as the White Park breed. Sadly, they are now listed as an endangered species; fewer than 450 cows remain.

Red kites are rare birds that breed in the moorlands and valleys of central and western Wales. The crowlike choughs thrive in Snowdonia National Park, along with peregrine falcons, merlins, and ring ouzels.

Badgering the Badgers

Badgers have been persecuted for centuries in Wales. Even the *Mabinogion*, an early collection of Welsh tales, tells about the mistreatment of badgers. Badger-baiting, or cruelly harassing badgers, was once a misguided form of sport. That's how the word *badger* came to mean "annoy," "heckle," or "abuse."

A badger, ready to hunt, emerges from his burrow.

Badgers are shy animals that emerge from their burrows to hunt at night. Historians suggest that people may have associated badgers with evil—the forces of darkness. At any rate, in 1973 the UK passed the Badgers Act to protect these animals. The next year, a group of Welsh badger-lovers formed the Gwent Badger Group to help ensure that the law was enforced.

Coastal Creatures

Seabirds such as razorbills, kittiwakes, guillemots, and puffins soar and dive along the coast. Many seabirds make their homes in colonies on the offshore islands. More than half of all the Manx shearwaters in the world nest on Skomer and Skokholm islands. One of the world's largest colonies of gannets lives on Grassholm. The Isle of Anglesey is another favorite gathering place for seabirds. Flocks of ducks, grebes, and warblers nest along Llangorse Lake in the Brecon Beacons.

Gannets nesting along the coast

The west coast is a breeding ground for gray seals. Large colonies of them live on Ramsey and Skomer islands. Skomer is also home to the Skomer vole, a little rodent that lives nowhere else in the world.

In Cardigan Bay, tourists may see bottle-nosed dolphins leap in graceful arches. This is one of only two locations in the United Kingdom where these intelligent, friendly creatures live. Conservationists are working hard to protect the dolphins and other marine life in Cardigan Bay.

A gray seal pup on the sandy shore

Princes, Saints, and Struggles

PEOPLE HAVE LIVED IN WALES FOR THOUSANDS OF YEARS. As early as 200,000 years ago, people were living in the caves of northern Wales. About 6,000 years ago, people from the European continent began migrating to Wales. They farmed and hunted, using tools they made from stone. They also erected gigantic stone monuments, or megaliths. Stone circles, called *cromlechs*, still stand at many sites in Wales today. A cromlech in Pembrokeshire was built of stones from the Preseli Hills of southwestern Wales. The megaliths used to build Stonehenge in England came from that same location.

Another wave of Europeans arrived around 2000 B.C. It's believed that they came from the Rhine River region of what is now Germany. These people, too, farmed and hunted. They knew how to make weapons and tools from bronze.

The Celts

Celtic people from Europe were next to migrate to Wales. By 500 B.C. they were well settled in. Many aspects of their culture have been passed down to today's Welsh people. The Celts were expert metalworkers and artisans. They made iron shields and swords, as well as beautiful jewelry. They adorned their artifacts with artistic designs of spirals and woven lines.

For defense, the Celts built hilltop forts. Their social system was divided into three main levels: warriors, Druids,

Opposite: **Ancient megalith erected almost 6,000 years ago in Wales.**

Celtic metalworkers crafted this bronze shield around 600 B.C.

and farmers. Druids, or priests, were selected from the warrior class, as were the kings. Some people believe the Druids built the huge stone monuments found throughout Great Britain. However, those were built long before the Druids' time.

The Celtic religion had many gods. Most of them were associated with animals, rivers, lakes, trees, and other things found in nature. Fantastic myths and legends grew up around the Celtic gods. These myths became the basis for Welsh tales that lived on for centuries. Many of these old tales were collected in the *Mabinogion* in the second century A.D.

Romans and Anglo-Saxons

Thousands of Roman soldiers began invading Wales around A.D. 50. Welsh tribes resisted them fiercely—especially the Silures of southeast Wales. Little by little, however, Wales fell to the Roman Empire. The Romans built roads, forts, and towns throughout the land. They found a wealth of minerals in Wales, too. The Romans mined gold in Carmarthenshire and copper in Anglesey.

The Romans finally left in the early 400s. At last, Welsh rulers and warriors had their lands to themselves—but not for long. For the next several hundred

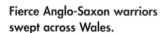
Fierce Anglo-Saxon warriors swept across Wales.

years, they fought off one wave of invaders after another. The most threatening opponents were the Angles and the Saxons, usually grouped together as Anglo-Saxons.

The legends of King Arthur began in this period. The real Arthur was a Welsh warrior who led his troops in a famous victory against the Anglo-Saxons around A.D. 500. Over time, King Arthur's reputation grew into a legend as history, religion, and myth blended together. Meanwhile, missionary monks were spreading Christianity throughout Wales. The best-known monk of all was Saint David, who became the patron saint of Wales.

Depiction of King Arthur conquering the Saxons

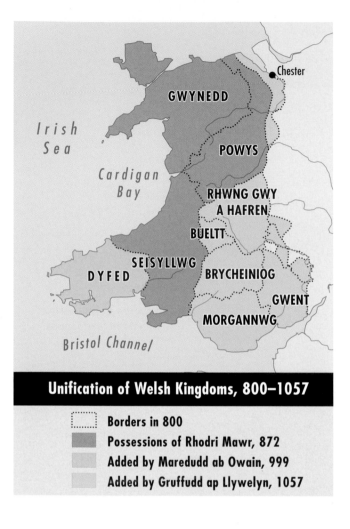

Unification of Welsh Kingdoms, 800–1057

- Borders in 800
- Possessions of Rhodri Mawr, 872
- Added by Maredudd ab Owain, 999
- Added by Gruffudd ap Llywelyn, 1057

An Anglo-Saxon chief named Offa ruled part of England in the 700s. Offa wanted to separate his kingdom from Wales. He dug a ditch with an earthen wall from the Dee River in the north to the Severn River in the south. That barrier was called Offa's Dyke.

The Welsh Princes

While the Anglo-Saxons were carving out their territory, Welsh leaders were forming domains of their own. These men became known as the Welsh princes. Some spent their reigns in petty battles with other princes. Others, often called Welsh kings, had visions of a united Wales. They built up powerful kingdoms. The greatest kingdoms were Gwynedd in the northwest, Powys in the northeast, and Deheubarth in the southwest.

Rhodri Mawr (Rhodri the Great) was the first to call himself king of the Welsh. In the 800s he became king of Gwynedd, Powys, and Seisyllwg. Together, they covered about half of present-day Wales. By uniting so much of Wales, Rhodri showed the Welsh that they could exist as an independent people.

Hywel Dda (Hywel the Good) was Rhodri's grandson. He united two kingdoms to create Deheubarth. When he joined it with Gwynedd and Powys in 942, he ruled most of Wales. He kept peaceful relations with England instead of waging war. Hywel also combined Wales's ancient legal traditions into one body of laws. Even by today's standards, these laws are models of common sense.

By 1063 Gruffudd ap Llywelyn united all the ancient Welsh kingdoms for the first time in history. Two more Welsh kings were to appear after the Norman conquest.

The Norman Period

In 1066, William the Conqueror invaded England and became its king. He had come from Normandy, a region of France. William stationed Norman nobles along the English–Welsh border to subdue the Welsh tribes. This border strip was called the Marches, and the Normans were called the Marcher lords. The Welsh fought long and hard against the Normans and their English allies.

It seemed that peace might reign in the time of Llywelyn Fawr (Llywelyn the Great). He united most

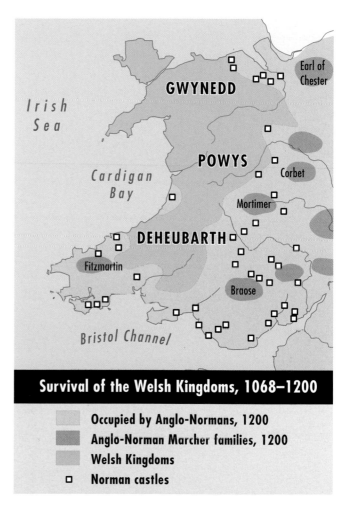

Survival of the Welsh Kingdoms, 1068–1200

- Occupied by Anglo-Normans, 1200
- Anglo-Norman Marcher families, 1200
- Welsh Kingdoms
- □ Norman castles

The Prince of Wales

of Wales, and the English kings accepted him as chief of the Welsh princes. England even made his grandson—Llywelyn ap Gruffudd—Prince of Wales. In 1282, however, he was killed in battle. He became known as Llywelyn the Last, because he was the last in a long line of great Welsh kings and princes. For a while, at least, Welsh resistance to England was over.

English Rule

After Llywelyn's death, King Edward I of England came down hard on Wales. With the Statute of Rhuddlan, he divided Wales into counties with English sheriffs in charge. The English built huge castles at Caernarfon, Conwy, Harlech, and other places. Only English people were allowed to settle in the towns around these castles, however. The Welsh became second-class citizens in their own country.

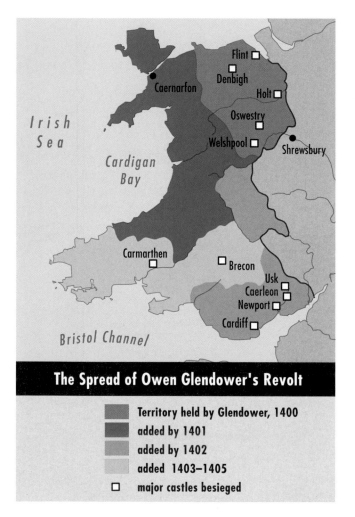

The Spread of Owen Glendower's Revolt

- Territory held by Glendower, 1400
- added by 1401
- added by 1402
- added 1403–1405
- □ major castles besieged

It was only a matter of time until the Welsh rebelled again, and Owen Glendower rose to the challenge. In 1400 he declared himself Prince of Wales. Then he stormed through the countryside, capturing one English castle after another. Owen wanted to unite Wales as an independent state. The revolt spread until, by 1405, all of Wales was united under Owen. However, he, too, met with defeat. Now England cracked down on Wales more harshly than ever. Welsh people were not allowed to hold office, own land in towns, or marry English citizens.

Owen Glendower

Owain Glyndŵr (Owen Glendower) (1359?–1416?) is a hero of Welsh nationalism. The rebellion he led against England in the early 1400s was Wales's last major effort to throw off English rule and become independent. Glendower established a Welsh Parliament and began his own foreign relations with other countries. Prince Henry (later King Henry V) eventually captured Glendower's castle fortresses at Conwy, Aberystwyth, and Harlech, thus breaking his power. No one knows what became of Glendower, and legends arose that he would return and lead Wales to victory.

King Henry VII

When Henry Tudor appeared, the Welsh believed they had a savior at last. Henry was part English and part Welsh, a descendant of Llywelyn the Great. Many saw Henry as the "second coming" of King Arthur or Owen Glendower—a champion for Wales in its struggle against oppression. In 1485, Henry gathered a Welsh army and defeated King Richard III of England at the Battle of Bosworth. However, things did not turn out as the Welsh people had thought. Instead, Henry became King Henry VII of England.

Union with England and the Landlord System

Henry's son, Henry VIII, passed the Act of Union in 1536. It made Wales "forever . . . incorporated, united and annexed to . . . England." The union was a mixed blessing for the Welsh people. They would have equal rights under the law, but now Welsh law was replaced by the English legal system.

Wales would also have representatives in England's Parliament. However, English—not Welsh—was now the official language in Wales. It's estimated that only about 5 percent of the Welsh people spoke English at that time. No one who spoke only Welsh could hold public office. As a result, a handful of English-speaking Welshmen rose to

Castles of Wales

Wales has countless castles. In the late 1200s, King Edward I of England built many of them as an "iron ring" of defense against Welsh resistance. Some of the more famous examples include:

Beaumaris Castle, on the Isle of Anglesey, was the largest of King Edward's castles. It was built in a perfectly symmetrical design, with the left and right sides matching. Invaders had to cross a moat, an outer wall, and a higher inner wall before reaching the courtyard.

Conwy Castle (below), with its eight gigantic towers, is joined to a massive wall that surrounds the entire town of Conwy. The town walls are 30 feet (9 m) high and 5.5 feet (1.7 m) thick. They were meant to protect the English townspeople from the native Welsh population.

Caernarfon Castle, with its unusual polygon-shaped towers, is one of Europe's greatest medieval fortresses. King Edward I intended to make it the seat of government in north Wales. His son Edward II—the first Prince of Wales—was born there. Today, each Prince of Wales is given the title at a ceremony in Caernarfon Castle.

Harlech Castle (above) stands high on a rocky cliff. A steep, fortified stairway leads down to the sea. It was Harlech's "stairway to the sea" at a time when the sea reached that far inland. In the 1460s, Welsh forces defended the castle against a seven-year English siege. That long siege gave rise to the heroic song "Men of Harlech." The song has become an unofficial anthem for Wales.

become upper-class gentry. They included members of Parliament, high sheriffs, judges, lawyers, and rich merchants.

The gentry, living in magnificent homes, took control of huge tracts of land across the countryside. Peasants who lived and farmed on their estates had to pay rent to their wealthy landlords. A peasant could be punished or even evicted from his farm for a variety of offenses. Resentment of the landlord system was to grow over the next 300 years.

The Anglican Church

England and Wales, like most of Europe, had been Roman Catholic countries. In religious matters, they were loyal to the pope in Rome, Italy. However, King Henry VIII of England broke with the pope over the question of divorce. Henry declared himself head of the Church of England, or Anglican Church. England and Wales were to unite under the new faith.

King Henry VIII, founder of the Anglican Church

All the monasteries and abbeys in Wales were closed. Their vast lands were transferred to the estate owners, along with the rents of their tenant farmers. Bishops and parish priests, who were unmarried, were replaced by Anglican clergy, who could marry. Devotions to beloved saints' relics and to pilgrimage sites came to a halt.

Ordinarily, church operations were supported by tithes. Tithes were required donations to a church of 10 percent of a parish member's income. However, after union with England, the tithes, too, went into the landlord's pocket. Some landlords took pride in their church buildings and kept them up, but most churches fell into ruins. Over the next 300 years, the Welsh Church became more and more poverty-stricken.

At this point, it seemed that Welsh language and culture were doomed to die out. However, events were soon to take a surprising turn. Welsh scholars insisted that to promote the Anglican faith, Wales needed Anglican prayer books in the Welsh language. And the English Parliament agreed. In 1567 both the Anglican *Book of Common Prayer* and the Bible were translated into Welsh. As a result, the Welsh language was preserved for centuries, when it might have died out altogether.

The Rise of Industrialization

Wales had always been rich in coal, iron ore, lead, copper, slate, and limestone. Before the 1500s, however, mining operations in Wales had been small. Then in the 1500s, mining began in earnest. By the late 1700s industrial mining had transformed the face of Wales. South Wales was the most heavily industrialized region. Merthyr Tydfil became the center of a booming iron industry. Huge coal reserves were exploited in the Swansea, Taf, and Rhondda valleys. Coal mines and slate quarries thrived in north Wales, too.

Slate quarries provided employment for many in North Wales.

In the 1800s canals were dug from the mines and quarries to the rivers. Then railroad lines were built from the mines to the seaports. Along the south and west coasts, shipbuilding became a booming industry. All these developments had one goal—to ship Wales's minerals and stone to markets around the world.

Riots and Reactions

Across the countryside, peasants dropped their plows and moved into the industrial towns. Living conditions were dreadful. They found ramshackle housing, dirty drinking water, low pay, and poor working conditions. An economic depression in 1829 made the workers' lives even worse.

Before long, riots broke out. The Merthyr riots of 1831 were the bloodiest industrial riots in British history. They lasted an entire month. Next came riots by the Chartists. This group wanted a charter granting the Welsh voting rights and equal representation in Parliament. More than 5,000 men marched on Newport, and soldiers shot dozens of them. Farmers in the countryside began staging the Rebecca Riots in 1839. They resented having to pay tolls as they moved their farm animals through the many tollgates. In the dark of night, men dressed up as women and destroyed the tollgates.

England's reaction to the riots was to suppress Welsh culture. Nonconformist religions were one target (see Chapter 8). Another was the Welsh language. In England's view, the people's inability to speak English was a major cause of the riots. If the Welsh could speak English, they could take part fully in life under English rule. In 1847 the government issued a report on education. The Welsh called it the Treason of the Blue Books. It declared: "The Welsh language is a vast drawback to Wales, and a manifold barrier to the moral progress and commercial prosperity of the people. It is not easy to overestimate its evil effects."

A natural reaction to the language ban was a rise in Welsh patriotism. Nonconformism spread faster than ever. Welsh-language societies began springing up, and some Welsh leaders began to push for self-government. In 1858 a Welsh cultural festival called the National *Eisteddfod* began. It gave Welsh people a chance to celebrate their traditional poetry, music, and dance.

Disasters, Unions, and Strikes

By the early 1900s the South Wales Valleys were producing one-third of the world's coal. The richest coal mines lay in the valleys around Newport and Swansea and the Rhondda Valley between Merthyr Tydfil and Cardiff. There were also iron mines in Merthyr and copper mines in Swansea. Hundreds of thousands of people worked in the mines, and thousands of immigrants poured into Wales for mining jobs.

Mining was dangerous work. The underground coal mines were not safe, and tragic mining disasters killed hundreds of people. In 1913, 439 miners were killed in an explosion at the Lancaster Pit near Caerphilly.

Workers clamored even louder for better working conditions. Soon, labor unions gave them a way to fight back. The labor unions were part of a growing socialist movement among Welsh workers. Socialists wanted not only better pay and safer conditions but also control—and even ownership—of the mines. Entire industries banded together to stage labor strikes, or refusals to work. Miners, quarry workers, and railroad workers went on strike throughout the early 1900s.

Industrial Death, Cultural Rebirth

An economic depression in the 1920s took its toll on Welsh workers. Hundreds of thousands of people lost their jobs. In the 1920s and 1930s, 750,000 Welsh people left Wales for other countries. Among those who stayed behind, as many as half the workers in the southern coal-mining valleys were unemployed.

By the mid-1900s Wales's industrial era was coming to an end. One by one, the huge coal mines shut down as the demand for coal dropped. Iron and copper mines and steel plants closed, too. The government took over the coal mines in 1947. This cut down on labor abuses, but most of the mines had to close anyway. Even in the 1990s unemployment in Wales hovered around 10 percent.

Hard times only made the Welsh more determined to preserve their culture and gain a stronger voice in their government. Little by little, their determination paid off. Welsh choirs and cultural clubs are stronger than ever now. Wales's own legislature met for the first time in 1999. The country is now officially bilingual, and the Welsh language is back in the schools.

Unemployed workers crowd the National Union of Seaman's offices.

The Welsh people are proud that they've been able to preserve their identity. Songwriter Dafydd Iwan expressed that pride in a song that's become a sort of second national anthem. It rejoices with a resounding chorus: "We are still here! We are still here! Despite everyone and everything, we are still here!"

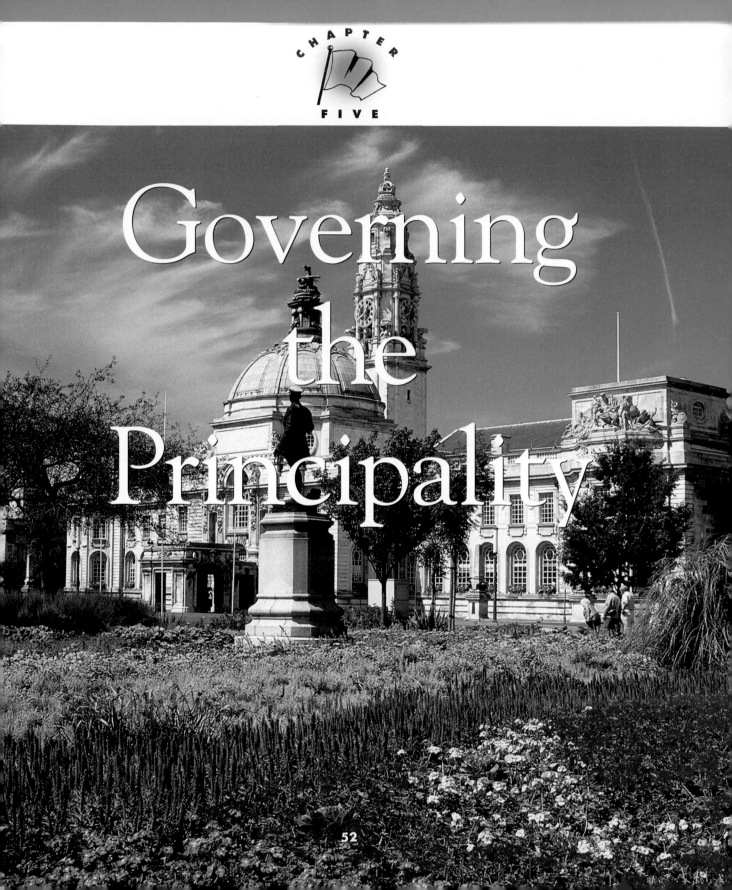

CHAPTER FIVE

Governing the Principality

F ROM A GEOGRAPHIC POINT OF VIEW, WALES IS PART OF THE island of Great Britain. It shares the island with England and Scotland. Politically, Wales is a principality within the United Kingdom, or UK. The UK's full name is the United Kingdom of Great Britain and Northern Ireland. Thus, the UK consists of England, Scotland, Wales, and Northern Ireland. (The terms *Britain* and *British* are often used to refer to the entire United Kingdom, however.)

Both Wales and Scotland gained a certain amount of self-rule in 1999. This changed the balance of power within the UK. But first, let's take a brief look at the UK's government.

Government in the United Kingdom

The UK is a constitutional monarchy. That means a king or queen is the head of state, and the British Constitution outlines the kingdom's governing principles. The Constitution, however, is not a single written document. It's a collection of statutes, common law, and traditions built up over hundreds of years. The British monarchy is hereditary—it passes from parent to child or to the next-closest relative as defined by law. Queen Elizabeth II has been Britain's monarch since 1952.

Opposite: **City Hall, Cardiff**

Queen Elizabeth II speaking at the annual opening of Parliament

Parliament is the UK's legislature, or lawmaking body. It is made up of two houses—the House of Lords and the House of Commons. Many countries around the world have used Britain's Parliament as a model for their own legislatures. Members of Parliament are informally called MPs.

The House of Commons is much more powerful than the House of Lords. Voters elect a total of 659 MPs to the House of Commons. Wales elects forty of those members. New Parliamentary elections, called general elections, must be held at least every five years. The House of Lords has about 700 members. Most of them are nobles, such as barons, earls, and countesses. Others are bishops and archbishops.

The UK's head of government is the prime minister. He or she is the leader of the political party that holds the largest number of seats in the House of Commons. The prime minister also appoints a number of cabinet ministers. They oversee important government departments such as health, education, and foreign affairs. The prime minister may call for a general election at any time—he or she does not have to wait for the five-year term to end.

House of Commons in session

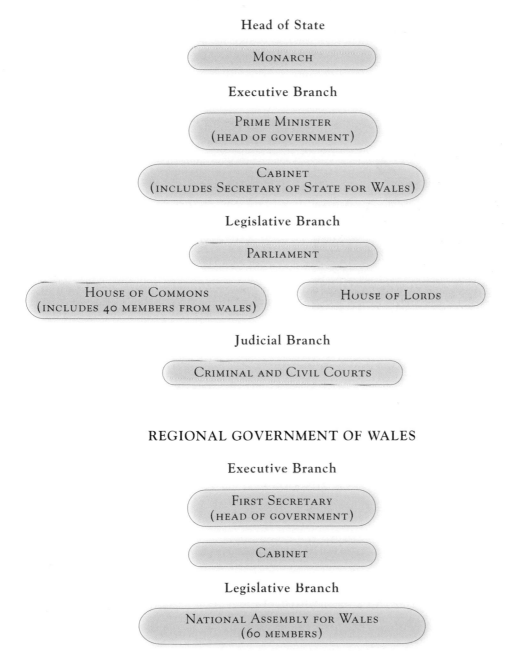

NATIONAL GOVERNMENT OF THE UNITED KINGDOM

Head of State

MONARCH

Executive Branch

PRIME MINISTER
(HEAD OF GOVERNMENT)

CABINET
(INCLUDES SECRETARY OF STATE FOR WALES)

Legislative Branch

PARLIAMENT

HOUSE OF COMMONS
(INCLUDES 40 MEMBERS FROM WALES)

HOUSE OF LORDS

Judicial Branch

CRIMINAL AND CIVIL COURTS

REGIONAL GOVERNMENT OF WALES

Executive Branch

FIRST SECRETARY
(HEAD OF GOVERNMENT)

CABINET

Legislative Branch

NATIONAL ASSEMBLY FOR WALES
(60 MEMBERS)

Wales's National Flag: The Red Dragon

A red dragon stands in the center of Wales's national flag. This dragon first appeared in Wales during Roman times. According to legend, King Arthur flew the red dragon flag. Then in the seventh century, the Welsh hero Cadwaladr carried the dragon standard into his battles. The dragon was clearly recognized as a Welsh symbol when Welsh archers flew the dragon flag at the Battle of Crécy in 1346.

Henry Tudor, the future King Henry VII of England, carried the dragon flag into the Battle of Bosworth Field in 1485. Henry later declared that the red dragon should be on Wales's official flag. In 1901 the dragon was recognized as the badge of Wales, and in 1953 it became the official Royal Badge of Wales and the authorized insignia for the Welsh flag.

In the background behind the dragon are two horizontal stripes, white and green. They are the official colors of the Tudor family.

Courts in the UK follow three slightly different legal systems. England and Wales follow one system, while Scotland and Northern Ireland each has its own. Some courts handle criminal cases; others deal with civil cases. For all three systems the House of Lords is the highest court, just as the Supreme Court is the highest U.S. court. Wales has no separate court system of its own.

Devolution: Home Rule at Last!

Devolution is the biggest news in Wales's political life today. But what does devolution mean? In short, it means home rule for Wales. Before devolution was passed, the British Parliament had almost total control over Wales's affairs.

It took Wales a long time to get to this point. A referendum for home rule was presented to Welsh voters in 1979. It turned out to be a great disappointment for supporters of home rule. About 80 percent of the voters said no. People in both North and South Wales suspected that the other region would dominate the government. However, events over the next eighteen years changed people's minds. During those years the UK's government was in the hands of the Conservative Party, which opposed home rule for Wales. The Labour Party, on the other hand, favored giving more power to the UK's political divisions. In 1964 the Labour Party set up the UK's Welsh Office, headed by a secretary of state for Wales.

At last, in 1997 the Labour Party won control in the UK again. Under Prime Minister Tony Blair, the new government pushed for devolution in Scotland and Wales in order to give these lands a bigger say in their own government. England tended to overpower the others because most of the UK's people and wealth are concentrated in England. Some leaders feared that the union might fall apart unless the smaller divisions gained some self-rule.

Welsh National Anthem: "Mae Hen Wlad Fy Nhadau"

Words by Evan James (1809–1878); music by James James (1833–1902). Unofficially adopted after its first public performance at the National Eisteddfod in Bangor in 1874.

Mae hen wlad fy nhadau yn annwyl i mi,
Gwlad beirdd a chantorion, enwogion o fri;
Ei gwrol rhyfelwyr, gwlad garwyr tra mad,
Tros ryddid gollasant eu gwaed.

Gwlad, Gwlad, pleidiol wyf i'm gwlad,
Tra mor yn fur i'r bur hoff bau,
O bydded i'r hen iaith barhau.

Hen Cymru fynyddig, paradwys y bardd,
Pob dyffryn, pob clogwyn, i'm golwg sydd hardd;
Trwy deimlad gwladgarol, mor swynol yw si
Ei nentydd, afonydd i mi.

Os treisiodd y gelyn fy ngwlad tan ei droed,
Mae hen iaeth y Cymry mor fyw ac erioed;
Ni llyddiwyd yr awen gan erchyll law brad,
Na thelyn berseiniol fy ngwlad.

"Land of My Fathers"
(First verse and chorus in English)
The land of my fathers, the land of my choice,
The land in which poets and minstrels rejoice;
Whose stern warriors were true to the core
While bleeding for freedom of yore.
Chorus:
Wales! Wales! Favorite land of Wales!
While sea her wall, may nought befall
To mar the old language of Wales.

(Translation by Ebenezer Thomas.)

In 1997, Wales held another referendum for home rule. The results were not exactly overwhelming. Only 25 percent of Wales's eligible voters cast their ballots. Even then, home rule won by a fraction of 1 percent. It was a narrow victory, but it was a victory all the same. As a result, Wales would have its first all-Welsh legislature since the days of Owen Glendower in 1404!

The National Assembly

Wales's first National Assembly convened in 1999. It has sixty members. Forty members are elected directly by the voters, while the other twenty are chosen according to political party. Each party's share of those seats depends on the percentage of votes it received in the last general election.

Since the National Assembly is so new, it has only limited powers. It has taken over the areas that used to be handled by the UK's Welsh Office. That's actually quite a range of responsibilities, however. They include education, culture, health, housing, roads, industrial development, local government, and law and order. In its early years, at least, the National Assembly cannot make laws or raise taxes. Wales is still part of the UK, so any laws passed in Parliament apply to Wales also.

Labour MP Alun Michael addresses the National Assembly, the first to sit in nearly 600 years.

Don't forget—Wales also elects forty MPs to serve in the UK's House of Commons. After understanding the flurry of excitement about Wales's new National Assembly, this can be confusing!

Wales's head of government is the first secretary, or first minister. He or she is the leader of the party that holds a majority in the National Assembly. Several other ministers make up the secretary's cabinet. They head ministries that oversee education, economic development, health and social services, the environment, and other important areas.

David Lloyd George

David Lloyd George, First Earl Lloyd George of Dwyfor (1863–1945), was the first British prime minister to have come from Wales. He was not born in Wales, but in Manchester, England. However, he came from a Welsh family and he grew up in Wales.

Lloyd George was a proud Welshman and a champion of Welsh causes. As a young solicitor, or lawyer,

he first made his name in the famous Llanfrothen Burial Case. His victory gave members of nonconformist religions the right to be buried in Anglican churchyards. In 1890 he was elected a Liberal Party MP from Caernarfon. He soon led the party's *Cymru Fydd* (Young Wales) movement for Welsh freedom and equality.

Lloyd George held his seat in Parliament for fifty-five years. He favored social reform and caused the House of Lords to lose its veto power on financial measures. His distaste for the House of Lords was no secret. In a speech he once described them as "Five hundred men, ordinary men, chosen accidentally from among the unemployed."

Lloyd George was a leader in the Liberal Party and served as prime minister from 1916 through 1922. He aggressively supported war against Germany in World War I (1914–1918) and helped bring about the peace treaty after that war.

The first secretary selects these cabinet members from the National Assembly.

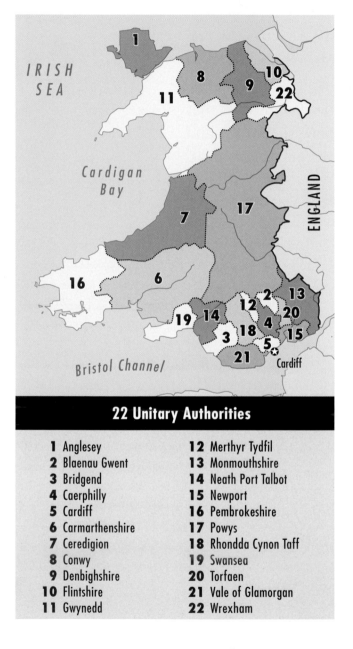

IRISH SEA

Cardigan Bay

Bristol Channel

Cardiff

ENGLAND

22 Unitary Authorities

1 Anglesey	**12** Merthyr Tydfil
2 Blaenau Gwent	**13** Monmouthshire
3 Bridgend	**14** Neath Port Talbot
4 Caerphilly	**15** Newport
5 Cardiff	**16** Pembrokeshire
6 Carmarthenshire	**17** Powys
7 Ceredigion	**18** Rhondda Cynon Taff
8 Conwy	**19** Swansea
9 Denbighshire	**20** Torfaen
10 Flintshire	**21** Vale of Glamorgan
11 Gwynedd	**22** Wrexham

Local Government

For a long time, Wales was divided into thirteen counties that were responsible for local government. In 1974 this system was changed to eight counties and subdivided into thirty-seven districts. Since 1996, Wales has had twenty-two local governing districts called unitary authorities. However, it's still common for people to think of the old eight or thirteen counties as historic and cultural divisions.

Each unitary authority is responsible for government services in its area. These include education, housing, social services, roads, and town planning. Voters in each area elect a council to supervise the unitary authority. The unitary authorities report directly to Wales's cabinet.

Political Parties

In terms of voter support, the Labour Party is Wales's leading party by far. It has a history of supporting South

Wales's miners and other working-class people. Most of Wales's representatives in Parliament are Labour Party members. Labour also won almost half the seats in Wales's first National Assembly elections.

Plaid Cymru is the national party of Wales. Its official name is Plaid Cymru–The Party of Wales. It promotes Wales's interests, and many party members hope that Wales will become a nation of its own. Many Welsh farmers support Plaid Cymru.

Welsh activists formed Plaid Cymru in 1925 when they realized that other British political parties were not supporting Wales. At that time, Plaid Cymru's goals were much the same as they are now—home rule and the preservation of the Welsh language.

Voters never sent more than a handful of Plaid Cymru members to the British Parliament. However, Plaid Cymru pressured other British political parties to create Welsh sections within their own parties. Plaid Cymru leaders continue to push for Welsh-language education and equal status for the Welsh language.

The Conservative Party aims to uphold the UK's government and constitution. It favors a strong economy based on free enterprise and personal responsibility. Conservatives have not strongly supported the movement toward devolution, because home rule runs counter to their belief in a strong central government. Naturally, Conservatives have only a small following in Wales. Still, they won nine seats in Wales's first National Assembly. Another party, the Liberal Democrats, is also active in Welsh politics.

Rhodri Morgan

Rhodri Morgan, as leader of the Welsh Labour Party, was the first person to become Wales's first secretary, or head of government, when the National Assembly convened in 1999. Born in 1939 in Cardiff, he was educated at Oxford University in England and Harvard University in the United States. Morgan headed the European Community Office in Wales (1980–1987) and represented the Cardiff West district in the British Parliament (1987–2001).

Cardiff: Did You Know This?

Population: 315,040 (Unitary authority, mid-1996)

Year founded: 1090

Average January Temperature: 40°F (4.4°C)

Average July Temperature: 61°F (16°C)

Cardiff is located on Wales's southeast coast. It sits at the mouth of the Severn, where the river empties into the Bristol Channel. The city began as a Norman fort in 1090. Over time, a huge stone castle was built, and the city grew up around the castle.

In the 1800s, Cardiff's port was the major shipping point for coal mined in South Wales. The mining valleys radiated out from Cardiff, and trains hauled the coal down to the city. There it was loaded onto ships bound for destinations around the world. Cardiff became Wales's official capital in 1955. It's also Wales's largest city, as well as its commercial and cultural center.

Massive Cardiff Castle (left) with its surrounding park, where peacocks strut and spread their glorious tail feathers, stands in the downtown area. Other historic buildings are two medieval churches—Llandaff Cathedral and Saint John's Church. Across from Saint John's, a huge indoor market sells farm products and traditional Welsh foods. Many government buildings stand in the Civic Centre. Nearby is the National Museum of Wales.

Coal is no longer unloaded at Cardiff's docks, but the waterfront is now renovated. Its gleaming new buildings stand in stark contrast to Cardiff's older sections. One new structure is Millennium Stadium, the city's new rugby stadium. Another ultramodern waterfront building will be the new home of the National Assembly, scheduled to open in 2004.

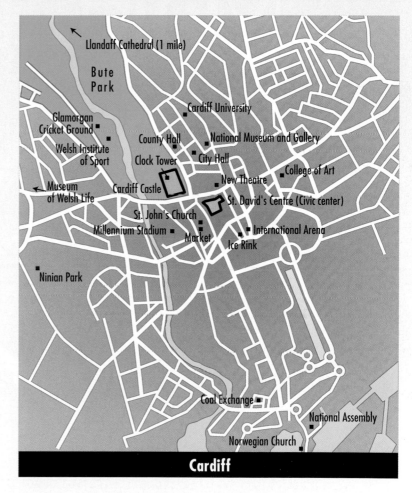

Cardiff

Making a Living

SIX HUNDRED YEARS HAVE PASSED SINCE OWEN GLENDOWER led a Welsh rebellion against England. But his cause and his memory live on. In the 1980s a Welsh group calling themselves *Meibion Glyndwr* (Sons of Glendower) set fire to holiday cottages in North and West Wales. It was a lawless act of violence, but they were protesting what they saw as a new kind of English oppression. The cottages had been purchased by English people from English real-estate agents who dealt in Welsh property. Thus, Welsh people were being excluded from their own land.

Many English people buy property in Wales because the cost of living there is lower than it is in England. Prices in Cardiff, for instance, run about 5 to 10 percent lower than those in London. In the countryside, prices are even lower. However, wages are lower in Wales, too. A Welsh adult who works full-time earns an average of £368 (US$531) a week. The average for workers in England is £416 (US$600) a week.

Actually, Wales is one of the poorest countries in Europe. The only regions in Western Europe with a lower standard of living are Spain, Portugal, Greece, and the former East Germany.

Opposite: **A farmer moves his cattle out to graze.**

Mining—Not What It Used to Be

Coal mining used to be Wales's major industry. From 1841 on, the number of coal miners in Wales increased every year. By 1921 more than 260,000 Welshmen were miners—almost

Coal mines were once a major source of employment in Wales.

10 percent of the entire population! Immigrants from Ireland, Italy, Germany, and Poland were pouring in to work in Wales's mines. Since then, however, the coal-mining industry has steadily declined, mostly because people began to use other energy sources.

Today, less than 1 percent of Wales's population works in the coal industry. Coal is still mined in the northeast and the south. The best coalfields are in southern Wales, stretching from Kidwelly to Cwmbran. Their coal deposits are extensive, and they yield high-quality anthracite coal. One old mine—Tower Colliery—was bought out by the miners, who proudly run it as a workers' cooperative.

Wales once had rich deposits of iron ore. However, they were eventually mined out. Oil is refined at Pembroke and at Milford Haven, one of Europe's leading oil-refining centers.

Several sites in Wales show what mining life used to be like. The Big Pit Mining Museum is in Blaenavon, and the guides there are former miners. They take visitors—all wearing protective hard hats—deep underground, through winding tunnels, to show them how miners used to work. At Llechwedd Slate Caverns, visitors venture into the deep caverns and chambers of this old quarry and watch slate-splitting demonstrations.

A worker splits slate at the Llechwedd Slate Caverns.

Blaenavon

The Welsh mining town of Blaenavon was named a World Heritage Site by the United Nations Educational, Scientific, and Cultural Organization (UNESCO) in 2000. It was designated as a world treasure "of outstanding universal value" for its role in Britain's Industrial Revolution. This town near Newport in the South Wales Valleys was home to the Big Pit colliery, or coal mine, and a huge ironworks. It was first developed in the late 1700s. Five furnaces, a foundry, a water-balance lift, and coal miners' houses still stand there. The Big Pit began operating around 1812 to supply iron and coal to the ironworks. It was closed in 1980 and opened as a museum in 1983. Today, it's the most popular coal-mining museum in Great Britain.

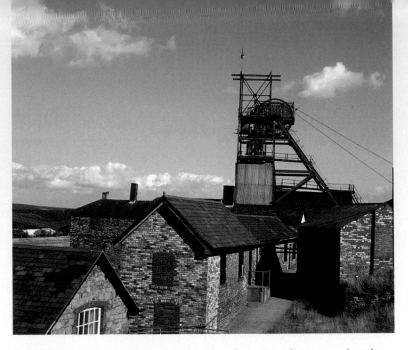

Agriculture—A Sheep-ish Business

Sheep- and cattle-raising are Wales's major farm activities. The sheep far outnumber the cattle. In 2000, Welsh cattle farmers had about 1.3 million cattle and calves. Sheep farmers, however, owned more than 11 million sheep and lambs!

Wales raises more sheep than any other area in Europe. Sheep graze on the hillsides and meadows across the rolling countryside, and farmers sell their

Sheep dot the hills of Snowdonia.

wool and meat. Wales's flatter lowlands and coastal areas are better for grazing cattle. The dairy industry is centered in southwest Wales. The dairy cows' milk is sold as packaged milk and processed into butter and cheese.

Barley, wheat, oats, and potatoes are the major crops. It's hard to raise other crops on a large scale because of Wales's climate and irregular land-scape. In fact, the European Union has designated about four-fifths of Wales's land as "less favored areas" (LFA), meaning the land is not well suited for agriculture.

One plan for raising Wales's farm income is organic farming, a natural, environment-friendly way to raise crops and animals. It involves using natural materials to fertilize crops, control pests, and keep the soil healthy. Farm animals are given nat-

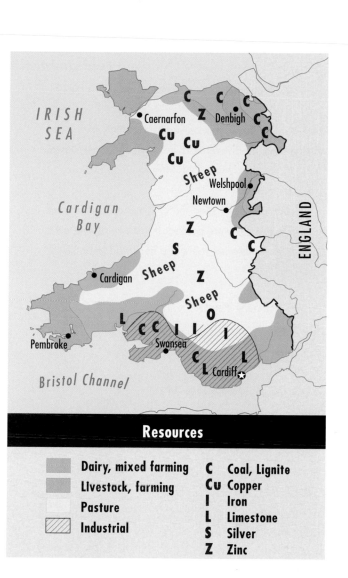

Resources

Dairy, mixed farming		C	Coal, Lignite
Livestock, farming		Cu	Copper
Pasture		I	Iron
Industrial		L	Limestone
		S	Silver
		Z	Zinc

ural feeds, and their health and comfort are priorities. Organic farming protects the air, water, and soil and recycles wastes. The National Assembly funds research and trains farmers in organic methods at the Organic Centre at the University of Wales in Aberystwyth. It is hoped that organic farming will make Wales's farm products more attractive in world markets.

Foot-and-Mouth Disease

In 2001 foot-and-mouth disease took a terrible toll on Wales's sheep and cattle. Throughout the spring and summer this highly contagious animal virus swept through Great Britain and Ireland. The government had to destroy millions of farm animals to keep it from spreading.

Clouds of smoke filled the countryside as diseased animal carcasses were burned. If just one animal on a farm had the disease, the entire herd had to be killed.

In many cases government agents destroyed not only infected herds, but also healthy herds on neighboring farms.

By June 2001 the sheep population was down by more than a million animals from the year 2000. By autumn the crisis was over, and people began to make plans to restock their herds. As one Welsh farmer said, "Raising animals is our life. It's in our blood. And sooner or later we'll go back to it."

Money Facts

The British pound sterling (£) was Wales's basic currency as of 2002. (That was the year when most countries in the European Union adopted the Eurodollar [euro] as their national currency.) A pound sterling is made up of 100 pence (p). Bank notes come in denominations of 5, 10, 20, and 50 pounds. There are also £-1 and £-2 coins. Other coins come in values of 50, 20, 10, 5, 2, and 1 pence. Queen Elizabeth II is pictured on most pieces of currency. In August 2002, £1 was equal to US$1.53 or 1.56 euros. US$1 was equal to £0.65 (65 p) or 1.02 euros.

Manufacturing

Manufacturing is the industry that brings the most money into Wales's economy. Many of Wales's manufacturing activities process and refine minerals. There are steel mills in Llanwern and Port Talbot, and Anglesey has aluminum-processing plants. Tin is processed into sheets in Llanelli.

Many foreign companies have opened factories in Wales. Today, about one-third of Wales's factory workers hold jobs in foreign-owned companies. The Japanese are among the

Manufacturing is a lucrative industry for Wales. Here is a view of a steel-smelting plant.

Weights and Measures

Like the rest of the UK, Wales uses the metric system. However, the imperial system is still in use in some areas. (The imperial system, also used in the United States, uses quarts, pounds, feet, miles, and so on, instead of the metric system's liters, kilograms, meters, and kilometers.) In Wales gasoline prices are quoted in liters, while highway signs usually show distances in miles.

What Wales Grows, Makes, and Mines

Agriculture (2000)

Sheep and lambs	11,192,200 animals
Cattle and calves	1,273,000 animals
Barley	123,000 metric tons
Wheat	110,000 metric tons

Manufacturing (1999) *(production value in pounds sterling)*

Metals and metal products	£1,324 million
Electrical and optical equipment	£1,215 million
Food products	£826 million
Chemical products	£745 million

Mining (1999) *(production value in pounds sterling)*

Mining and quarrying (including iron ore, oil, and gas)	£360 million

biggest investors in Welsh manufacturing, with more than sixty Japanese firms investing. Foreign-owned factories are especially active in high-technology industries. They make electronic and electrical equipment, automotive parts, aircraft engines, and chemical products. Other factories produce food and beverage products, metal products, plastics, and artificial fibers.

Tourism and the Economy

Service industries bring in more than half of Wales's income. Almost two-thirds of Welsh workers hold service jobs. Service jobs include banking, government work, health care, and education. They also include hotels and other businesses that serve tourists.

Tourism is an important source of income for Wales. Tourists enjoy visiting Wales's castles, seashores, and national parks. In the process, they support hotels, guest houses, restaurants, museums, and shops. Many small- and medium-sized businesses depend almost entirely on tourist income.

A trekker takes a long walk along Offa's Dyke.

For both tourists and locals, trekking through the countryside is a favorite activity. Unfortunately, walking trails were closed during the foot-and-mouth disease outbreak in 2001. People could easily carry the disease on their shoes from one farm to another. As a result, tourists stayed away from Wales for months, and the impact on the economy was severe.

Wales and the European Union

The UK joined the European Community in 1973. That organization later changed its name to the European Union (EU). The EU is an organization of European countries that cooperate in the areas of trade and economic development. Member countries contribute to the EU's funds and receive aid in return. The EU also makes it easy for members to trade with one another.

Like many other people in the UK, the Welsh were not sure about the advantages of belonging to the EU. They were afraid the UK would lose its cultural identity and its decision-making power. As a result, the UK held onto its pound-sterling currency instead of changing to the EU's Eurodollar, or euro. Still, EU membership has been good for Wales in many ways. Today, the Welsh National Assembly decides how EU funds are spent.

EU funds are invested in road-building and city-redevelopment projects. The EU provides loans to help small businesses and to start new companies in Wales. It also helps promote tourism and develop recreation areas. And the EU has given Wales a whopping grant of almost $2 billion to fight poverty.

Thanks to its EU membership, Welsh companies have also been able to open branches in other EU countries. The EU's regulations for environmental protection make sure that no member pollutes the air and water of another member across borders. EU workplace standards also give basic employment rights to Welsh workers, as well as to others across Europe.

The Severn Bridge connects Wales and England.

Getting Around Wales

A little ferry used to take people across the Severn River between England and South Wales. A small bridge opened in 1966, but over time, it could no longer handle the heavy traffic. Finally, in 1996 the Severn Bridge opened—the longest bridge in Great Britain. The M4 motorway runs across it, then follows Wales's southern coast. As soon as drivers cross the bridge, they know they're in Wales. A big sign greets them with the friendly message, *Croeso i Cymru*—Welcome to Wales.

Most roads in Wales are well-paved, two-lane routes. In some parts of the countryside, however, roads are so narrow that they are, in practical terms, one lane. An oncoming car has to pull over to let the other car pass. On a winding road that clings to a steep mountainside, this can be a hair-raising experience! In the winter, ice and snow make it almost impossible to travel in higher elevations. Mountain roads are often closed when driving conditions become too dangerous.

Old steam locomotives pull many of Wales's tourist excursion trains. These trains used to haul slate from mountain quarries to seaport cities. A railway preservation society began reviving steam trains for passenger use in the 1950s. Now many of them run through Snowdonia National Park and other scenic areas.

A well-paved but narrow country road.

Two preserved rail lines start off from the town of Porthmadog. The older of the two is the Ffestiniog line, which started up in 1860. It passes through a luxuriant valley of oak forests and rhododendrons. The Vale of Rheidol railway, beginning in Aberystwyth, takes its passengers on a spectacular ride. It speeds up high inclines, around hairpin curves, and along steep, overhanging ledges.

Sightseers love taking the train that goes up Snowdon Mountain. It leaves from Llanberis, at the foot of the mountain. It's an exciting trip—but it's also a frighteningly steep climb. When this railway made its first run in 1896, the engine tumbled into a ravine. No accidents have occurred since then, however. The reward for riders' bravery is a beautiful view of the countryside.

Passenger trains connect many cities and towns. British Railways also operates many rail lines in Wales. Some offer high-speed train service to London and back, although there is no train line between North and South Wales. One line follows a scenic route along the Cambrian Coast. Passengers pass beaches, sand dunes, and wild, rocky coasts. They rumble over bridges and cling to steep cliff sides. Most luxurious of all is the Black Prince. Its cars once belonged to the famous Orient Express.

Several ferries cross the Irish Sea between Wales and Ireland. Their terminals in Wales are at Holyhead, Pembroke, Fishguard, and Swansea. The main ocean port is Milford Haven, one of Europe's major centers for importing oil.

Cardiff has an international airport. Its airlines

The charming Snowdon Mountain Railway takes visitors to the top of the mountain.

connect with other big cities in the UK and many points on the European continent. *Awyr Cymru*, Wales's national airline, flies from Cardiff and Swansea to Dublin and Cork in Ireland.

Getting the Word Out

The British Broadcasting Corporation (BBC) began operating in Wales in 1937. It provides radio and television service in both English and Welsh. The Welsh were never quite satisfied with BBC Wales, though. They felt its broadcasts were slanted toward an English point of view and did not represent Wales's culture and interests. The Welsh began campaigning for their own television station, even staging noisy protests in front of the BBC offices in Wales.

At last, in 1982 the Welsh station S4C was established. S4C stands for *Sianel Pedwar Cymru* (Channel Four Wales). About thirty hours of programs a week are broadcast in Welsh. Its programs come from the BBC; from Wales's independent broadcasting company, HTV; and from many small, independent companies. One of its most popular programs is a nighttime soap opera called *Pobol y Cwm* (*People of the Valley*). S4C's broadcasts are doing a lot to encourage the use of the Welsh language.

The BBC's Radio Cymru broadcasts more than 120 hours a week in Welsh. Other radio service in Welsh comes from smaller companies such as Radio Ceredigion and Swansea Sound.

The *Western Mail* is Wales's national daily newspaper. Many people in North Wales read the *Liverpool Daily Post*, which has several Welsh-language columns.

Proud to Be Welsh

Celtic people began settling in Wales more than 3,000 years ago. While they struggled against invasions by Romans, Anglo-Saxons, and Normans, they held on to their language, culture, and pride. The Welsh people today still take pride in their Celtic roots. They refuse to give up the language and culture for which their ancestors fought so hard.

It's difficult to describe a whole nation of people. However, the Welsh have a reputation for being warmhearted, outgoing, and neighborly. When they run into strangers, they're open, welcoming, and generous. They also take pride in their villages and homes and feel a strong attachment to the place where they live.

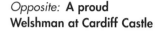

Opposite: **A proud Welshman at Cardiff Castle**

A group of friends enjoy each other's company.

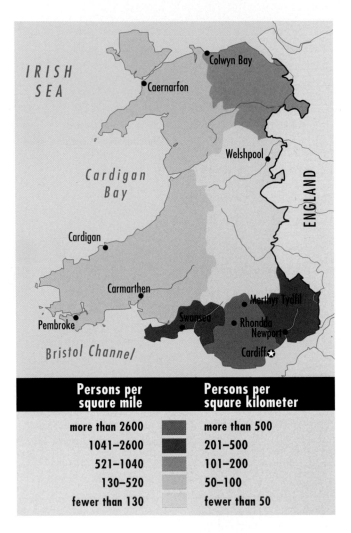

Persons per square mile		Persons per square kilometer
more than 2600		more than 500
1041–2600		201–500
521–1040		101–200
130–520		50–100
fewer than 130		fewer than 50

Population of Major Cities
(mid-1996 unitary authority figures)

Cardiff	315,040
Swansea	230,180
Newport	136,789

Only about 500,000 people lived in Wales in the mid-1700s. With the industrial boom of the 1800s, however, the population exploded. Immigrants arrived from England, Ireland, Spain, Italy, and other countries. By 1921 the population was about 2.6 million. In 2000, Wales was home to about 3 million people.

About three-quarters of the Welsh people live around the large cities and mining valleys of South Wales. The largest cities are Cardiff, Swansea, and Newport. All three grew as ports that once shipped out coal and iron.

Cardiff, the capital, is an outward-looking, European-oriented city, with communities representing many cultures. For example, it has a 200-year-old community of people who originated in the African country of Somalia. Spanish-speaking people make up another large community in Cardiff. Still, Cardiff has a large concentration of Welsh speakers.

The overwhelming majority of Welsh residents belong to white ethnic groups. Ethnic minorities make up only about 1.5 percent of the population. They include South Asians from India, Pakistan, and Bangladesh. Others belong to

Chinese and other East Asian cultures. Some minorities come from Africa, the Caribbean, and other lands.

Regional Differences

In the United States, the North and the South have their own distinct history, character, and outlook. In Wales, the difference between regional cultures is even greater. South Wales grew into an industrial region, with big-city business centers. People of many nations and cultures immigrated to the southern towns. As industry grew and the population became more diverse, English became the popular way to communicate.

Wales is home to a number of ethnic minorities.

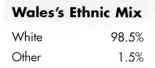

Wales's Ethnic Mix

White	98.5%
Other	1.5%

A busy, modern shopping mall in Cardiff.

Grazing sheep and stone cottages can be seen throughout rural North Wales.

Meanwhile, North Wales remained largely a farming region. Without an influx of foreigners, Welsh was always the dominant language. Northerners came to see the south as an English region. The real difference, however, was in the two regions' way of life. South Wales had an urban, working-class society, while North Wales had a rural lifestyle.

In spite of their differences though, North and South Wales were both truly "Welsh"—but in different ways. South Wales was not as English as it seemed to northerners. Middle-class city dwellers adopted many English customs, but Welsh ways were very much alive in the mining valleys. Native Welsh people were the first to work in the coalfields. There they set up Welsh chapels, societies, trade unions, and work-men's institutes. Even though they learned English, many also held onto their Welsh language. When they did speak English, native Englishmen could easily tell they were Welsh.

In time, many features of southern culture were embraced throughout Wales. The game of rugby, for instance, began in the south. Today Wales's rugby teams are a source of national pride. *Pobol y Cwm* (*People of the Valley*) is Wales's most-watched television series. It's set in a working-class southern town. Poet Dylan Thomas and singers Tom Jones and Shirley Bassey came from South Wales. All Welsh people are proud of these stars.

One of the oldest languages in Europe, Welsh is spoken by 19 percent of the people.

The Welsh Language

Wales has two official languages—English and Welsh. Welsh is a Celtic language. The Celts were powerful tribes who once inhabited much of Europe. As the Roman Empire expanded across Europe most Celtic dialects gradually gave way to Latin-based languages. In Wales, however, the language survived, though it picked up many Latin influences.

Today, Welsh is one of the oldest spoken languages in Europe. Its nearest relatives are Cornish (of Cornwall, England) and Breton (of the Brittany region in France). More distant "cousins" are Scottish Gaelic and Irish Gaelic. Modern Welsh is a direct descendant of the early Welsh spoken in the sixth century A.D.

The Welsh Alphabet

Letter	Pronunciation
a	short: as in ham
	long: as in hard
b	b as in boy
c	k as in kin
ch	breathy *kh* as in Bach
d	d as in dog
dd	th as in the
e	short: as in get
	long: as in hey
f	v as in love
ff	ff as in off
g	hard g as in got
ng	ng as in sing
h	h as in hat
i	short: as in sit
	long: ee as in seen
j	j as in jam
l	l as in lamp

Letter	Pronunciation
ll	(place tongue in *l* position and blow air past it)
m	m as in man
n	n as in not
o	short: as in gone
	long: as in more
p	p as in pet
ph	ff as in off
r	r as in rat
rh	*hr* (blow out breath)
s	s as in sit
t	t as in top
th	th as in thin
u	short: i as in sit
	long: ee as in seen
w	short: oo as in look
	long: oo as in fool
	consonant: w as in wind
y	short: i as in sit or u as in hut
	long: u as in put or ee as in seen

Road signs in Wales are in both Welsh and English.

The basic Welsh alphabet has twenty-eight characters. A twenty-ninth letter—*j*—has been added to adapt to the many English words that use it. Welsh has no *k, q, v, x,* or *z.*

To someone who does not speak Welsh, the language can look alarmingly difficult. So many *w*'s and *y*'s and double letters! But it's not so hard as it looks. There are so many *w*'s and *y*'s because these are two of the seven vowels in Welsh. The double letters—*dd*, *ff*, and *ll*—are really separate alphabet characters, like separate letters, with their own sounds.

Young children have an easier time learning to read Welsh than learning to read English. In English, many letters are not pronounced, and many letter combinations are pronounced differently in different words. But in Welsh, every letter is pronounced, and their sounds are usually the same.

A Welsh scholar, Peter Williams, wrote the following message to help English speakers read Welsh. The message is in English, but it uses Welsh spellings to represent the sounds. See if you can read it!

"Gwd lwc. Ai hop ddat yw can ryd ddys and ddat yt meiks sens tw yw. Iff yw can ryd ddys, dden ywar dwing ffaen and wil haf no problems at al yn lyrnyng awr ffaen Welsh alffabet."

In English, it reads: "Good luck. I hope that you can read this, and that it makes sense to you. If you can read this, then you are doing fine and will have no problems at all in learning our fine Welsh alphabet."

If you can read the message, you are well on your way to reading Welsh! As you see, it only takes a little practice.

Common Welsh Words and Phrases

S'mae (smy)	Hello
Hwyl (hoo-eel)	Good-bye
Sut dach chi? (sit dakh kee?)	How are you?
Iawn, diolch (ee-ow-n, dee-olkh)	Fine, thanks
Os gwelwch yn dda (oss gwe-look 'n tha)	Please
Diolch (dee-olkh)	Thank you
Faint? (vye-nt)	How much?
Ie (ee-yay)	Yes
Na (nah)	No
Cymru (kum-ree)	Wales

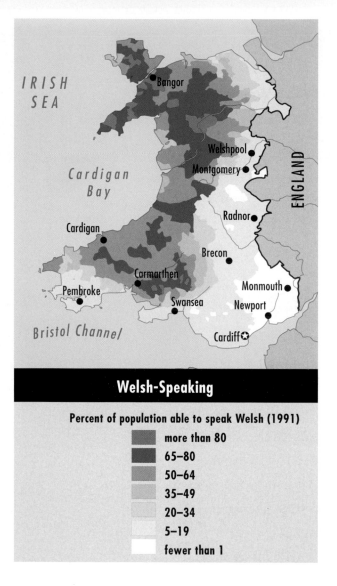

Welsh-Speaking

Percent of population able to speak Welsh (1991)

- more than 80
- 65–80
- 50–64
- 35–49
- 20–34
- 5–19
- fewer than 1

Keeping the language alive is one of the major themes in Welsh life today. In the 1850s about 75 percent of the Welsh people spoke Welsh. By the early 1900s this figure had dropped to about 50 percent. Today, only about 19 percent of Welsh people speak the language. Most Welsh speakers live in the rural areas of north and west Wales. Welsh is their first language—the language they use in business, government, and everyday conversation.

Welsh speakers are a growing group though. Welsh-language societies began springing up as soon as Welsh was banned from schools in the 1870s. In the twentieth century, pro-Welsh groups continued to pressure the government for language rights. Little by little, they made headway. In 1993 the British Parliament passed the Welsh Language Act, making Wales officially bilingual. At last, Welsh was on an equal footing with English.

Meanwhile, more and more schools were giving bilingual classes and even all-Welsh classes. As a result, the number of young people who speak Welsh has been growing fast. Welsh-language radio and television shows have helped, too.

Broadcasting, education, government, and many industries now need more bilingual employees. And job hunters are finding that bilingual skills give them a better chance of landing a job.

The Name Game

Certain first names that people use outside Wales are Welsh in origin. Welsh female names include Meredith, Gwyneth, Glynis, and Riannon or Riana. Some Welsh names for males are Gareth, Dylan, Lloyd, Owen, Cedric, Clyde, and Rhys or Reece.

Jones is the most common surname in Wales. Almost 14 percent of the population has the name Jones! Williams is next, with 9 percent, followed by Thomas and Evans. This can get confusing, as any one town might have several residents named John Jones or Will Williams.

To keep everyone sorted out, the Welsh often give people clever nicknames. A tailor might be called Jones the Stitch, while a fisherman would be Jones the Fish. Tommy Up and Down might have one leg shorter than the other, while Will Straight Back walks erect. In one Welsh village, there were two men named Evans—a travel agent and a funeral director. The townspeople called the travel agent "Evans There and Back" and the funeral director "Evans One Way"!

Just Say "Llanfair PG"

In northwest Wales, on the island of Anglesey, is the village of Llanfairpwllgwyngyll-gogerychwyrndrobwll-llandysiliogogogoch. Each part of the name has a meaning. The full translation is "The church of Saint Mary, in the hollow of the white hazel, near the rapid whirlpool and the church of Saint Tysilio near the red cave."

Actually, the town's original name was the much shorter Llanfair Pwllgwyngyll. Around 1850 a local shoemaker added the rest of the name. He wanted to give his hometown some distinction, since a newly built railroad bridge made the village less popular as a train stop. In 1988 the village council officially returned the name to its shorter form, but the long name is still seen all over town. Informally, people just call the village Llanfair PG.

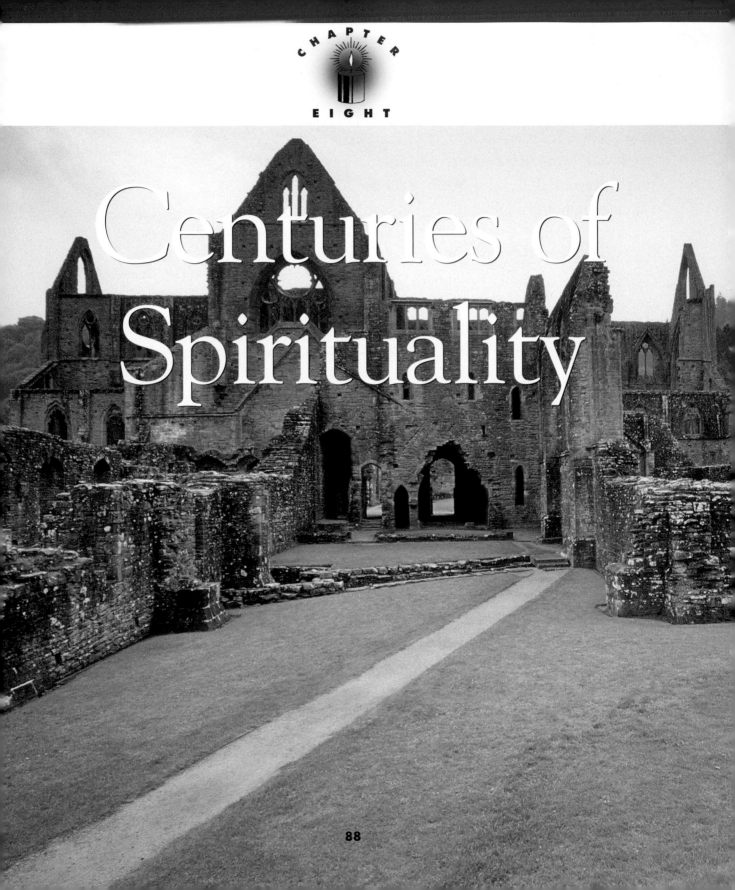

Centuries of Spirituality

CHRISTIANITY MADE ITS WAY INTO WALES DURING ROMAN times. By the seventh century, missionary monks had converted all the people in Wales to Christianity. Abbots presided over the monasteries, while exceptional monks became bishops. When the pagan Anglo-Saxons invaded, the Welsh held even more strongly to their religion.

Wales maintained its own version of Christianity, called the Celtic Church. Meanwhile, Christians in the rest of the Western world were Roman Catholics. Saint Augustine became the Catholic archbishop of Canterbury in England in 597. He asked the bishops in Wales to conform to Roman Catholic practices, but they refused. The main issue seems a small one; it concerned how to set the date for Easter. Finally, in the 1100s, the Archbishop of Canterbury gained authority over Christians in Wales.

Reminders of the Celtic Church are seen all over Wales today. For example, hundreds of place names begin with *Llan*, meaning "enclosure." The name comes from a time when Welsh princes donated land to the church, and monks

Opposite: **The twelfth-century Tintern Abbey**

Ruins of an abbey in Llangollen

Major Religions in Wales

Denomination	Membership*
Church in Wales (Anglican)	90,000
Roman Catholic	83,500
Presbyterian (Calvinistic Methodist)	44,900
Independent	36,200
Baptist	24,300
Methodist	16,600
United Reformed	4,300

*2000 est. Note: Figures can be misleading because different denominations may record their statistics differently.

enclosed the land with religious buildings. These religious compounds often included study centers, monks' quarters, and a church. Eventually, *Llan* referred to the enclosures, their churches, and the villages that grew up around them. Towns named *Llanfair* are especially common. *Llanfair* means "Saint Mary's Church." The word *Mair* means "Mary," but when joined to the prefix *Llan*, it becomes *fair*.

The Age of Saints

The sixth and seventh centuries are known as Wales's Age of Saints. During this time missionary monks built churches, monasteries, and schools throughout Wales. The monk-historian Gildas wrote about these monks in A.D. 540, calling them *sancti*, a Latin word meaning "holy ones." This was translated as "saints"—hence the name Age of Saints.

The monks led lives of prayer and self-discipline. By their good example and through their teaching, they won the respect

Celtic crosses mark many graves and holy sites in Wales.

of even the tribal princes. Many miracle stories grew up about the saints, too, and they were credited with miraculous cures. The wells in some saints' churchyards were known as holy wells for the healing power of their waters. Holy wells, stone crosses, and inscribed memorial stones were known as "relics of the saints." Several place names in Wales begin with *Merthyr*, meaning "relic."

Each saint preached over a wide area and gained devout followers. Saint Tysilio's territory in Powys surrounded his monastery and church at Meifod. Saint Deiniol preached in eastern Wales, and Saint Padarn covered mid-Wales. Saint Beuno is considered the patron saint of North Wales. His center was on the Lleyn Peninsula, and his territory spread across North Wales and the Isle of Anglesey.

Saint Cadfan founded several churches on Wales's west coast. Then he retired to Bardsey Island, off the tip of northern Wales, and founded a monastery. So many monks were buried there that Bardsey became known as the Island of 20,000 Saints. The island became a popular place for pilgrimages, and many people wanted to be buried there, close to the saints. Saint Gwyddfarch was a monk who preferred an isolated life of prayer. He built a hilltop dwelling in the Vyrnwy Valley, where he lived until he died.

A chapel on Bardsey Island

Saint David's Cathedral

Saint Illtud is known as the father of the Welsh saints. He had many disciples, and his great monastery and learning center in the Vale of Glamorgan was named *Llanilltud Fawr* (Llantwit Major). It's sometimes called Britain's first university. Among Saint Illtud's students were Gildas, the historian, and Saint David, the patron saint of Wales.

Dewi Sant (Saint David) is the most beloved of all the Welsh saints. Churches throughout Wales are named after him, so he probably preached far and wide. He founded a monastery on the southwest tip of Wales, near the town now called Saint David's. The massive Saint David's Cathedral and Bishop's Palace stand there today. March 1, the day he died, is celebrated as Saint David's feast day.

Many miracle stories grew up around Saint David. He is said to have cured one of his teachers of blindness. Several tales tell of wells springing up where he preached. His most famous story took place at Llanddewibrefi in southwest Wales. David attended an assembly of bishops there. When he began to speak, the land beneath him rose up, lifting him so high that everyone could hear him.

Saint David

Saint David, the patron saint of Wales, was known for his holiness, self-denial, and tireless missionary work. He founded a monastery on the southwest tip of Wales and was a powerful force in spreading Christianity. More than fifty churches in Wales are named after him, most of them in the south. Stories of Saint David's miracles and good works abound. By the ninth century he was called *Aquaticus*, from the Latin word for "water," because he and his monks were said to have lived on only water. His earliest biography was written in the eleventh century. It says that he founded ten monasteries and that his monks were vegetarians. Among all the Welsh saints, Saint David is the only one who was canonized—declared a saint—by the Roman Catholic Church.

Not all the Welsh saints were men. Saint Winefride, the niece of Saint Beuno, was said to have been martyred by beheading. Where her head fell, a well of healing waters sprang from the ground. Saint Beuno built a church over the spot, and Saint Winefride's Well became a famous pilgrimage site at Holywell in North Wales.

Saint Melangell, the daughter of a Scottish king, pledged herself to God. When her father insisted that she marry, she fled to Powys in Wales. When a hare the prince of Powys was hunting ran to Melangell for safety, the prince was very impressed. He gave Melangell a gift of land, where she started a religious community for women.

Anglicanism and the Welsh Language

When Wales and England united in 1536, the Anglican Church became Wales's official religion. The *Book of Common Prayer* was the prayer book for Anglican Church services then, as it is today. By 1567 both the prayer book and the Bible's New Testament were translated into Welsh. This was a great victory for Welsh language and culture. In practicing their religion, the Welsh people were able to hold on to their language, their Celtic roots, and their sense of being a separate people.

The Welsh scholar William Morgan came out with a translation of the entire Bible in 1588. Morgan followed the style of early Welsh poetry, especially the ballads. Thus, ordinary Welsh people were educated in their native literary style as they read the Bible. It's no wonder that poetry became a natural form of expression for them.

Resentment of the Anglican Church still boiled beneath the surface though. Many people thought Anglicanism was the same as the landlord system. They saw it as just another oppressive institution forced upon them by England.

As early as the 1600s, some people in England and Wales began to reject Anglican teachings. They were called Nonconformists, or Dissenters. One group was the Quakers, who gained many converts in Wales. They held the shocking belief that God could be known through an inward light, with no need for ministers, creeds, or churches. The Quakers were eventually forced out of England and Wales and settled in the United States, mostly in Pennsylvania.

At the same time, small gatherings of Baptists and Congregationalists began to meet in Welsh villages. Both followed a strict code of conduct in their personal lives. Today, Baptists believe that God's word is revealed in the Bible and that each local church has the authority to interpret the Bible. Members are baptized upon professing their repentance and faith.

Congregationalists believed that each congregation had the right to make its own rules and decisions, without any higher authority. They were often called Independents. That name is still used for some congregations in Wales. Meanwhile, other Congregationalists united with similar churches in England and Scotland. Today, they're grouped as the United Reformed Church.

Nonconformism and the Methodist Revival

Nonconformist beliefs were a direct assault on the authority of the Anglican Church. But once they began, they found eager followers in Wales. The Methodist Revival was to be a powerful force.

The Methodist religion arose in Wales in the mid-1700s. At first, Methodism was just a revival movement within the Anglican Church. One early leader in Wales was Howel Harris. He experienced a religious conversion in 1735 and began founding Methodist groups in Wales. Over time, Methodism grew more and more popular among the people. Eventually, most Welsh Anglicans joined the movement.

Methodism in Wales finally made a formal break with the Anglican Church. The Anglican minister Thomas Charles started many Methodist groups throughout Wales. In 1811 he ordained several people as Methodist ministers. From that point on, Methodism was a separate religion in Wales.

Methodism took a different course in Wales than it did in England. Methodists in England followed the teachings of John Wesley, who taught that grace was freely available to all. Wesley's followers became the Methodist Church in England. Wesley's form of Methodism has followers in Wales today, but most Welsh Methodists preferred the teachings of the Frenchman John Calvin.

Calvin believed in *predestination*—the idea that God decides who is to be saved. This version came to be called the Calvinistic Methodist Church, or the Presbyterian Church of Wales. Calvinistic Methodism was a stark contrast to Anglican practices. Anglican churches were highly decorated, and services were stately rituals. There were many levels of church officials. Calvinistic chapels, on the other hand, were plain and simple. Leaders were not far removed from worshipers, and services often consisted of preaching and hymn-singing in the Welsh tradition.

The Church in Wales

When the Methodist Revival took place, some people in Wales wanted to remain Anglican. Their congregations were called the Church in Wales. Although they were Anglican, they considered themselves separate from the Church of England. With the Welsh Church Act of 1914, the Church of England formally recognized the Church in Wales as independent. This took effect in 1920. After that, its membership grew.

For both Anglicans and Roman Catholics, the primary worship service is a celebration of the Eucharist. The heart of the service is the consecration of bread and wine into the body and blood of Christ, in memory of the Last Supper. The faithful then receive these in Communion, showing their union in Christ. Several prayers and scripture readings lead up to the Eucharist service. *The Book of Common Prayer* contains the Anglican worship services and prayers.

The Archbishop of Wales oversees the Church in Wales's six dioceses, or geographical divisions. Even though it's governed separately, the Church in Wales is part of the Anglican Communion, which also includes Anglicans in England and Scotland.

Celtic Religion Before Christianity

The Celtic people and their religion stretched across Europe in pre-Roman times. Celtic religious practices flourished not only in England and Wales but also in Ireland. The Celts believed in life after death. Thus they buried food, weapons, and other useful objects with the dead. They also believed in transmigration, which is similar to reincarnation—that is, they believed that a soul could migrate into another living being, either human or animal, after death.

Druids collect mistletoe, which grew on the sacred oak trees.

Druids were the priests of the Celtic religion. Their name means "knowing the oak tree," and they conducted religious rituals in the forest. As keepers of the calendar, they announced when crops were to be planted. They also held religious festivals, cared for religious shrines, and conducted rituals. Today, the Druids are cultural and patriotic symbols in Wales.

The Druids were also learned men. Some of them studied for years and memorized thousands of verses of poetry. However, they never put these verses in writing. When Christianity arrived, this tradition of learning fit in well with scholars in the monasteries. Christian monks were the first people to write down Wales's ancient Celtic myths.

Land of Poets
and Singers

WELSH BARDS, OR SINGING POETS, WERE WEAVING THEIR enchanting spells as early as the sixth century A.D. Their favorite subjects were brave kings and valiant warriors with lofty ideals. Their poems had complex sound patterns, with repeated consonants and rhymes within lines. This grew into the traditional Welsh form of poetry called *cynghanedd*.

Taliesin and Aneirin are Wales's best-known early bards. Taliesin wrote songs of praise for the ideal ruler, who was brave in battle and generous in peacetime. Aneirin is best known for the *Gododdin*, about a band of noble warriors. Their valiant deaths assured them of everlasting glory.

The Gorsedd of Bards—an association of poets—first met in 1792. It was instituted by Iolo Morganwg, an eccentric Welsh scholar. He wanted to reinforce the point that the Welsh were direct descendants of Celtic culture. So, he styled the Gorsedd as a Druid order, linking it with the Druid priests of ancient Celtic times. Today, people who have made a significant contribution to Welsh culture are invited to join

Opposite: **Wales's great poet Dylan Thomas**

The Gorsedd of Bards

the Gorsedd. Members include writers, musicians, and even politicians and rugby stars!

The Arthur Legends

The tales of King Arthur and the knights of the round table are well-known British legends. Many historians believe Arthur originated in Wales. The ninth-century historian Nennius called Arthur "a leader of battles, who defeated the Saxons twelve times." Nennius says Arthur and his warriors met and rallied in the Welsh town of Caerleon. The ruins of a large, round amphitheater stand today in Caerleon. These ruins could be the inspiration for Arthur's legendary meetings with his knights of the round table.

In the 1100s the Norman-Welsh author Geoffrey of Monmouth began to shape Arthur into the person we know today. He wrote tales about a wise and noble king who ruled in a golden age before the Saxons invaded. King Arthur, he said, carried a magical sword named Caliburn, which was forged on the Isle of Avalon.

Geoffrey's tales and other Celtic and Welsh legends soon fell into the hands of a French poet named Chrétien de Troyes. Chrétien polished these tales up and turned them into long, narrative poems. They became wildly popular throughout France, Germany, and Britain.

The Mabinogion and Celtic Legends

The *Mabinogion* is a collection of eleven Welsh tales based on Celtic mythology and folklore. It was first written down in the 1000s. The tale "Kulhwch and Olwen" contains many details of the Arthur legend. Kulhwch's cousin Arthur helps him in many of his adventures. Arthur's men include Kei—the source of Sir Kay—and Gwalchmei—who became Sir Gawain.

One figure in the *Mabinogion* is Rhiannon, a horse goddess. She appears on a mysterious, pale horse and marries King Pwyll of Dyfed, a land with a magic cauldron of plenty. Another figure is Lleu, one of the most honored gods in Celtic Wales. Then there's Brân, a gigantic god whose severed head kept his companions joyful and safe.

Ceridwen was a goddess often pictured as an old hag. She had a very ugly son named *Afagddu*, meaning "utter darkness." Ceridwen wanted Afagddu to be accepted in fine society, so she boiled up her cauldron of inspiration. If Afagddu drank of this brew, he would become a wise and gifted poet. However, a servant accidentally drank the brew first, and Afagddu never got any. After many transformations, the servant ended up becoming the Welsh poet Taliesin—and thus begins Wales's real-life history as a land of poets.

The Royal National Eisteddfod is an annual celebration of Welsh culture. ("Eisteddfod" is pronounced *eye-STETH-vod*.) It's said that Lord Rhys held the first eisteddfod at his castle in Cardigan in 1176. He invited poets and musicians from all over Wales. A special chair at the lord's table was reserved for the best performer. In the years to come, many Welsh noble-men held eisteddfodau (the plural form) on their estates.

In 1860 the National Eisteddfod of Wales became an annual festival. Today, it's Wales's biggest cultural event and the largest folk festival in all of Europe. It's held in August,

Minstrels perform at the National Eisteddfod festival.

and the location alternates between North and South Wales. Thousands of poets, playwrights, novelists, musicians, artists, and architects compete in the weeklong festival, with all events conducted in the Welsh language. The high point of the festival is the "chairing" of the winning poet. He or she is awarded an ornate hand-carved chair, recalling Lord Rhys's prize. The Gorsedd of Bards plays a big role in every Eisteddfod. Members wear ceremonial robes, and their leader, the Archdruid, announces the poetry prizes.

Besides the National Eisteddfod, regional eisteddfodau are held around the country throughout the year. There's also an International Eisteddfod in Llangollen every July. The Welsh League of Youth holds its own eisteddfod in May. This organization is a nationwide social club for young people. It promotes the Welsh language through magazines, camps, and many smaller local events.

Choirs and the Cymanfa Ganu

In 1193 a writer noted that the Welsh people "do not sing in unison like the inhabitants of other countries, but in many different parts." Choirs and part-singing in harmony are old Welsh traditions, and one of Wales's many nicknames is "The land of song."

In the 1830s people began holding hymn-singing meetings in chapels. Choirs from neighboring towns soon began to band together for choir festivals. Many chapels held an annual *Cymanfa Ganu* (hymn meeting). They sang in four-part harmony, expressing plenty of *hwyl*, or Welsh-style emotion.

Many chapels, villages, and even rugby clubs throughout Wales have choirs. Some specialize in *penillion* singing, in which a harp plays the melody while the choir sings harmony.

Hay-on-Wye

Hay-on-Wye is known for having the world's largest collection of bookstores. More than thirty bookshops line the streets. Each one has its specialty, from brand-new issues to secondhand paperbacks to rare volumes. The town hosts its famous Literature Festival in early summer. It attracts some of the world's leading authors.

Dylan Thomas

Dylan Thomas (1914–1953), born in Swansea, is considered to be Wales's greatest modern poet. His verses are rich with images and luscious sounds. Before being recognized as a poet, he wrote newspaper articles, film scripts, and radio plays. Poetry was his greatest love, though, and at age twenty he published *Eighteen Poems*, his first book of poetry. He was to publish three more poetry collections and several short stories. Thomas died at age thirty-nine while on a lecture tour in the United States. Today, a simple wooden cross marks his grave in Laugharne, Wales.

Modern Welsh Celebrities

It's been said that the Welsh will "run a mile before they'll listen to a dull speaker." That may be a bit extreme, but the Welsh appreciate dramatic expression—whether it's spoken, written, or sung. Naturally, Wales has produced many poets, novelists, actors, and singers.

Dylan Thomas was the poet who wrote "A Child's Christmas in Wales," "Do Not Go Gentle into that Good Night," and many other beloved poems. Richard Llewellyn's novel *How Green Was My Valley* tells a heartrending story of coal-mining days in South Wales. R.S. Thomas, a poet-priest, wrote of the harshness of farmers' lives. And Saunders Lewis was both a playwright and a political activist.

Above left: **Anthony Hopkins**

Above right: **Catherine Zeta-Jones**

Tom Jones

Sir Richard Burton and Sir Anthony Hopkins are the most famous Welsh actors of all time. Both show how powerful the spoken word can be. Younger Welsh actors include Catherine Zeta-Jones and Ioan Gruffudd.

Tom Jones was Wales's most famous popular singer for decades. The son of a coal miner, he shot to stardom in the 1960s with his rough, powerful voice. Shirley Bassey is a Welsh singer with African roots. Charlotte Church is a young Welsh girl with a powerful, mature singing voice. The Welsh National Opera has produced many world-class opera stars, including the late Sir Geraint Evans, Dame Gwyneth Jones, and Bryn Terfel.

The National Museum and Gallery

The National Museum and Gallery stands in Cardiff's Civic Centre. No other museum in Great Britain has such a wide range of art and science displays.

One section takes visitors on a 4,600-million-year journey through time. Animals and plants of Wales's seashores and woods are displayed in the natural-history rooms.

Other exhibits feature Bronze Age gold objects, Celtic treasures, and early Christian monuments, as well as fossils and minerals. The Glanely Gallery is a hands-on area where visitors can explore collections that are usually hidden away. The art galleries show paintings by some of the world's greatest artists, such as Monet and Van Gogh.

The Stereophonics perform at the Cardiff International Arena.

Cool Cymru is a term that began popping up in Wales in the late 1990s. It refers to the explosion of fresh, new talent that brought Wales into the international cultural scene. Welsh rock bands such as the Manic Street Preachers, Catatonia, Gorky's Zygotic Mynci, and the Stereophonics draw huge crowds outside Wales. Welsh rock music with all Welsh lyrics, is more and more popular among young people. The National Eisteddfod even has a category for rock music!

Another new talent is fashion designer Julien Macdonald, who grew up in Merthyr Tydfil. He first became famous for

Love Spoons

Wooden love spoons are a traditional Welsh craft. They arose from the custom of giving someone a carved wooden spoon as a token of love. The handles are carved in intricate designs and patterns to symbolize special feelings. A handle in the shape of a key means "My home is your home." An anchor design means "With you I can stay and settle down." Two interlocking hearts mean "Our hearts are entwined forever."

designing clothing for the Spice Girls rock band. In 2001 he joined Givenchy, the French fashion house. Yet another new celebrity is filmmaker Justin Kerrigan. His first feature film, *Human Traffic*, was released in 2000, when Kerrigan was only twenty-five. It follows five young deadbeats through a wild weekend in Cardiff.

Folk Customs and Superstitions

The *Mari Lwyd* (Gray Mare) is an old Christmas tradition. It's a pre-Christian custom that's still followed in some parts of Wales. The leader puts on a horse's skull, complete with false ears, marble eyes, and movable jaw, and drapes a sheet around his body. Then he and his band of merrymakers go from door to door, clacking the horse's jaw and reciting insulting poems.

Another Christmas custom was the *plygain*. This was a gathering of men singing carols in harmony in the wee hours of Christmas morning. Beforehand, families made toffee by boiling the sugary liquid over an open fire and dropping dollops of it into icy water. The toffee ended up in all kinds of shapes. If you

The tradition of Mari Lwyd was common in the early 1900s.

made a piece of toffee that looked like a letter, that letter would be the initial of your future spouse!

Drinking from the wassail bowl was also a delightful custom at Christmas. An ornate, many-handled wassail bowl was filled with fruit, cakes, and spices and topped with warm beer. It was passed around the table, and each person who took a swig made a wish for everyone's good fortune in the coming year.

Good wishes abound for everyone when drinking from the wassail bowl.

Hunting the Wren took place on Twelfth Night, or January 5, the twelfth day of Christmas. A group of men went out, captured a wren, and put it in a decorated cage. Then they went from door to door and showed the wren in exchange for food or gifts.

Noson Lawen (Merry Night) celebrated the end of the hay harvest. Everyone gathered to dance, drink, recite poetry, and sing to the strains of a harp. Many villages throughout Wales still hold a Noson Lawen in their town halls.

Nos Galan Gaeaf was the night when the spirits of the dead walked about. In Celtic tradition, it was celebrated on the eve of the new year. With the coming of Christianity, it moved to All Hallows' Eve—October 31. People lit huge bonfires across the countryside to keep the spirits away. They roasted potatoes and apples in the flames and danced merrily around the fire for good luck. Once the fire died down, everyone scurried home quickly to escape the spirits.

Many superstitions surrounded the winter holidays. The Yule log had to be kept burning in the fireplace through the twelve days of Christmas. Lighting a new fire during that time would bring bad luck. Then the ashes from the Yule log had to be buried in the garden to assure a plentiful crop.

It was bad luck if your first visitor on New Year's Day was a redhead. It was also unlucky to lend anything, even a candle, to anyone on New Year's Day. And if you owed anyone money at New Year's, you would be in debt all year long—a warning that's still good today!

Everyday Life
in Wales

FARMHOUSES DOT THE COUNTRYSIDE IN RURAL WALES. SOME are large, rambling, two- or three-story houses, while others are simple stone cottages. Sheep graze on the hillsides around small family farms, and life is quieter and gentler there than it is in the cities. In the rural villages of north and west Wales, visitors are likely to hear Welsh spoken on the streets and in the shops.

Over the years, more and more people have left the farming areas for city jobs. Young people today tend to head for the cities, too. In larger cities, many people live in apartments in public-housing developments. Terrace houses, or row houses, are a common sight in the southern valleys. They are homes attached to one another and built in long rows.

Opposite: **An old shepherd's cottage is a home for those who prefer a slower lifestyle in Wales.**

Attached homes, or row houses, in Rhondda

Many Welsh people enjoy the local pub.

> ## *Leisure Time*

What do Welsh people like to do in their spare time? A survey in the late 1990s found that their most popular leisure activity was visiting the pub! Next came taking part in sports, and gardening was another favorite pastime. About one-third of the people in the survey enjoyed regular outings to the seaside or the country. Playing bingo, watching sports, and going to movies were also popular.

Wales is a great place for walking, and it has an extensive network of footpaths. Some of the toughest walks go up the rocky slopes of Mount Snowdon or through the Brecon Beacons. For long-distance trekkers, the Pembrokeshire Coast Path and Offa's Dyke Path provide quite a workout. The Pembrokeshire Path passes along rugged cliffs and sandy beaches and through tiny fishing villages. Other long walking paths are the Cambrian Way and Glyndwr's Way. Many footpaths in Wales were closed in 2001 to prevent the spread of foot-and-mouth disease.

Walkers enjoy a coastal footpath.

Millennium Stadium

Cardiff's Millennium Stadium opened in 1999. Some people call the glistening, ultramodern stadium the symbol of the new Wales. It overlooks the River Severn in Cardiff's riverfront redevelopment zone.

The stadium seats 72,500 spectators—50 percent more people than the stadium it replaced. It has a retractable roof that can be opened or closed, depending on the weather. Two huge screens at opposite ends of the stadium give spectators a magnified view of events. On any given day, they might see rugby, soccer, or boxing matches, as well as opera or rock concerts.

Rugby players need a natural-grass playing surface, so grass is grown off-site and brought into the stadium when needed. Every once in a while, a falcon is released to fly around the stadium and keep Cardiff's pigeon population at bay!

Sports

Rugby is Wales's favorite sport, and rugby stars are hailed as national heroes. Rugby is a rough, fast-moving contact sport, similar to soccer and American football. Players kick, pass, run, and tackle—protective gear is optional and they get no time-outs.

Wales's professional "ruggers" compete with teams around the world. At home, they play in Cardiff's new Millennium

Wales's captain Robert Hawley runs with the ball during the 1998 Five Nations Championship match.

Playing Fishes

Fishes is a popular playground game in Wales. To play, one person is "on" (that means "it"), and the rest of the players split into three teams. Each team gathers in one corner of a four-cornered space and chooses the name of a fish for their team.

The person who's on stands in the middle and calls out fish names. When the name of a team's fish is called, team members all take off running for the empty corner. The one who is on tries to "tip" them—that is, tag them. Whoever makes it to the empty corner without being tipped is the winner and gets to be on the next time.

Stadium. On match days, the police close the roads in Cardiff's main shopping area to make way for the crowds of fans. Everyone waits for the Big Match—the annual rugby face-off between England and Wales. The Wales-Scotland match draws another huge crowd.

The Rugby World Cup tournament is held every four years, and Wales hosted the games in 1999. The Welsh team made it to the quarter-finals before losing to the Australians, who ended up winning the cup.

Soccer, called football in Wales, is another favorite sport. Wales has a national professional team, as well as hundreds of amateur players. Cricket is popular, too. It's a ball game played with a flat bat and a red leather ball. National teams also represent Wales in golf, hockey, swimming, gymnastics, bowling, boxing, and athletics (track and field).

Going to School

Children in Wales have the same educational requirements as children in England. They are required by law to attend school from ages five through sixteen. Primary school lasts

Children gather round for lessons in a Welsh classroom.

from ages five through eleven, and secondary school goes on until students are sixteen.

All public schools generally follow Great Britain's national curriculum. It outlines what subjects students should study and what standards they should achieve. Schools have courses in Welsh history and also the Welsh language. Students take national tests at ages seven, eleven, and fourteen to see if they're up to par for their level.

Some students leave school at sixteen, while others continue at some level. Those who want to go on to college attend tertiary school, a type of post-sixteen high school. Others may study at a technical college.

Annual Holidays in Wales

New Year's Day	January 1
Saint David's Day	March 1
Good Friday	Varies: March or April
Easter Monday	Varies: March or April
Early May Holiday	First Monday in May
Spring Holiday	Monday, late May or early June
Late Summer Holiday	Last Monday in August
Christmas Day	December 25
Boxing Day	December 26

Welsh-language education is available at all levels, from preschool through secondary school. In fact, Welsh is now a required subject for all students from ages five through sixteen. They may learn it in a Welsh-speaking school or study it as a second language. Welsh-speaking schools are defined as schools where more than six subjects are taught in Welsh. In the 2000–2001 school year, more than 25 percent of Welsh children were attending Welsh-speaking schools.

The University of Wales was formed in 1893 by uniting colleges in Aberystwyth, Bangor, and Cardiff. The university system grew even bigger when it added three colleges in Swansea, one in Lampeter, and a College of Medicine in Cardiff. Other colleges include the University of Glamorgan and Trinity College in Carmarthen.

Welsh Rarebit

(Makes one serving)

Ingredients:

1 thick slice of bread

4 ounces grated hard cheese

3 tablespoons milk

2 teaspoons mustard

1 ripe tomato, sliced

Directions:

Lightly toast the bread. Then mix the cheese, milk, and mustard and spread it thickly over the toast. Cook it under a broiler or grill until the cheese mixture begins to bubble and turn brown. Remove from heat and put a few slices of tomato on top. Reheat briefly, then serve with the remaining tomato slices.

Eating in Wales

Welsh rarebit is Wales's traditional snack food. It's a sort of open-faced, grilled-cheese sandwich. Some people call it "Welsh rabbit," although that name has an unpleasant history. Unkind English people used to call it Welsh rabbit to make fun of poor Welsh people who could not afford to eat real rabbit!

Laver (pronounced "larver") bread is a typical breakfast food in Wales. It's a seaweed pancake made from a red seaweed found off Wales's southwest coast. The seaweed is boiled for hours, then mixed with oatmeal, formed into small cakes, and fried in hot bacon fat. It's often served with bacon.

Many people in Wales follow the British custom of afternoon tea. Usually served around 4:00 in the afternoon, it's a time to relax and enjoy a cup of tea and a light snack during the long stretch between lunch and dinner. Typical teatime snacks are *bara brith*, *bara claddu*, and Welsh cakes. Bara brith (speckled bread) is a rich fruit bread glazed with honey and often served with cheese. Bara claddu (pronounced "clathee") is a moist fruitcake with raisins and currants inside. Welsh cakes are little round cakes cooked on a griddle and sprinkled with powdered sugar.

Ladies enjoying teatime

Lamb pie and salt duck are served at this restaurant.

Welsh lamb is the traditional meat for dinner. Glamorgan sausages are not made with meat, though, but with grated cheese, bread crumbs, and chopped leeks. They're usually served with potatoes. *Cawl* is a country stew made of meat and vegetables—usually potatoes, carrots, leeks, and onions. The seasoning depends on the cook. Cheese and butter from country farms have always been important in the Welsh diet.

Traditional Dress

People in Wales today dress like people do in other Western countries. In earlier times, however, they wore a distinctive style of clothing. The Welsh national costume was created in the early 1800s. Lady Llanover, an iron manufacturer's wife, encouraged Welsh people to wear it to stress their cultural identity. She won a prize at an eisteddfod in 1834 for her essay on preserving Welsh language and dress, and she certainly practiced what she preached. She had all the servants on her South Wales estate wear her idea of the national costume. Other Welsh people followed suit, feeling that their national identity was in danger of becoming extinct.

Women wore a black felt hat with a high crown and a wide brim. Beneath the hat they wore a lace cap. They also wore a striped flannel petticoat covered by a long skirt of black-and-white checks. This, in turn, was covered with a starched white apron. A red cloak was draped over the shoulders. Proper ladies also wore black woolen stockings and black shoes. Some Welsh men still wear a traditional muffler (scarf) and a coal miner's cap. These costumes and other Welsh clothes worn over the centuries are on display at the Museum of Welsh Life near Cardiff.

Welsh folk dancers wear traditional dress at their performances.

The Museum of Welsh Life

The Museum of Welsh Life is an open-air museum on the grounds of Saint Fagan's Castle, just outside Cardiff. It shows how Welsh people have lived, worked, and played since Celtic times. Dozens of original buildings have been moved here from all over Wales. They include houses, a school, a chapel, and craftsmen's shops. Indoor exhibits include costumes and household and farming implements, and there are daily demonstrations of traditional craft-making and farm chores. At the museum's annual Christmas fair, people follow traditional Welsh holiday customs.

The biggest family celebrations of the year are Christmas and Easter. While traditional customs still flourish in some parts of Wales, a modern family usually gathers for a big holiday dinner. Birthdays and weddings are important occasions, too.

Christmas morning in Wales

When a boy or girl turns eighteen, it calls for a special celebration. When they reach eighteen, they're entitled to vote and have the legal rights of an adult.

A traditional wedding

Wales's national holidays are the same as England's. Boxing Day, December 26, is a traditional holiday in Great Britain and many other countries. It has nothing to do with fighting though! It's named for the tradition of giving small boxed gifts to servants and less fortunate people on the day after Christmas. Today, however, Boxing Day is mostly a day to relax and unwind after Christmas.

National holidays that fall on weekdays are often called "bank holidays" because the banks are closed that day. Shops and schools are closed, too. Some bank holidays don't celebrate any occasion—it just seems like a good time for a break! They always fall on a Monday, making for a nice three-day weekend. Wales has May, spring, and summer bank holidays.

Saint David's Day—March 1—honors the beloved patron saint of Wales. It's not an official holiday in Wales, but the Welsh people are trying to get it officially approved. Meanwhile, schools celebrate the day with music festivals, and people wear their leeks and daffodils. In their hearts and minds, they're never far from their proud heritage of poets, singers, princes, and saints.

Timeline

Welsh History

People from the European mainland begin migrating to Wales.	**c. 4000** B.C.
Bronze Age people, probably from the Rhine River region of Germany, begin arriving in Wales.	**c. 2000** B.C.
Celtic people are well established in Wales.	**c. 500** B.C.
Roman invasion of Great Britain begins.	**c.** A.D. **50**
Anglo-Saxon invasions begin.	**c. 400**
Saint David establishes a monastery in southwest Wales.	**c. 550**
Celtic folk legends are written down in the *Mabinogion*.	**1000s**
William the Conqueror becomes king of England; Norman rule begins.	**1066**
Welsh resistance to England ends with the death of Llywelyn ap Gruffudd.	**1282**
King Edward I of England names his son Edward II Prince of Wales.	**1301**
Owen Glendower begins a revolt that spreads throughout Wales.	**1400**
Henry Tudor (the future King Henry VII) defeats King Richard III in the Battle of Bosworth.	**1485**
King Henry VIII passes the Act of Union, uniting England and Wales.	**1536**
The Bible and the Anglican *Book of Common Prayer* are translated into Welsh.	**1567**

World History

2500 B.C.	Egyptians build the Pyramids and the Sphinx in Giza.
563 B.C.	The Buddha is born in India.
A.D. **313**	The Roman emperor Constantine recognizes Christianity.
610	The Prophet Muhammad begins preaching a new religion called Islam.
1054	The Eastern (Orthodox) and Western (Roman) Churches break apart.
1066	William the Conqueror defeats the English in the Battle of Hastings.
1095	Pope Urban II proclaims the First Crusade.
1215	King John seals the Magna Carta.
1300s	The Renaissance begins in Italy.
1347	The Black Death sweeps through Europe.
1453	Ottoman Turks capture Constantinople, conquering the Byzantine Empire.
1492	Columbus arrives in North America.
1500s	The Reformation leads to the birth of Protestantism.

Welsh History

The Methodist Revival in Wales begins.	1735
Wales's Industrial Revolution begins as mining becomes the major industry.	Late 1700s
Workers' riots sweep through Wales.	Early 1800s
Mining industry expands in the southern coalfields.	1850–1900
The first National Eisteddfod is held.	1858
The University of Wales is chartered.	1893
An explosion at the Lancaster Pit near Caerphilly kills 439 miners.	1913
Disestablishment of the Anglican Church in Wales.	1920
Cardiff becomes Wales's official capital.	1955
The Welsh Language Act allows Welsh in legal and official contexts.	1967
The UK joins the European Community (later renamed the European Union).	1973
The Welsh radio station—S4C— begins broadcasting.	1982
A new language act gives Welsh equal status with English.	1993
Wales's first National Assembly convenes.	1999
The mining town of Blaenavon is named a World Heritage Site.	2000
Foot-and-mouth disease devastates Wales's sheep and cattle farms.	2001

World History

1776	The Declaration of Independence is signed.
1789	The French Revolution begins.
1865	The American Civil War ends.
1914	World War I breaks out.
1917	The Bolshevik Revolution brings communism to Russia.
1929	Worldwide economic depression begins.
1939	World War II begins, following the German invasion of Poland.
1945	World War II ends.
1957	The Vietnam War starts.
1969	Humans land on the moon.
1975	The Vietnam War ends.
1979	Soviet Union invades Afghanistan.
1983	Drought and famine in Africa.
1989	The Berlin Wall is torn down, as communism crumbles in Eastern Europe.
1991	Soviet Union breaks into separate states.
1992	Bill Clinton is elected U.S. president.
2000	George W. Bush is elected U.S. president.

Fast Facts

Official name: Principality of Wales (Welsh: Cymru)

Capital: Cardiff

Official languages: English and Welsh

The waterfront at Swansea

Wales's flag

Glacier carved valley

Religion:	No state religion; major religions are Church in Wales (Anglican), Methodism, Nonconformist denominations, and Roman Catholicism
National anthem:	*Mae Hen Wlad Fy Nhadau* ("Land of My Fathers")
Government:	Constitutional monarchy
Head of state:	Monarch of the United Kingdom of Great Britain and Northern Ireland
Head of government:	National: British prime minister Wales: First Secretary
Area:	8,015 square miles (20,758 sq km)
Borders:	England to the east, the Irish Sea to the northwest, Saint George's Channel to the west, the Bristol Channel to the south
Highest elevation:	Mount Snowdon, 3,561 feet (1,085 m) above sea level
Lowest elevation:	Sea level along the coast
Largest island:	Anglesey, 276 square miles (715 sq km)
Average annual precipitation:	42 inches (107 cm) in Cardiff
Average January temperature:	40°F (4.4°C)
Average July temperature:	61°F (16°C)
Length of coastline:	614 miles (988 km)
Greatest distance, north-south:	137 miles (220 km)

Harlech Castle

Currency

Greatest distance, east-west:	116 miles (187 km)
Major rivers:	Severn, Wye, Dee, Clwyd
Largest natural lake:	*Llyn Tegid* (Bala Lake)
National population (2000 est.):	2,946,200
Welsh-language speakers (1991 est.):	18.7 percent

Population of major cities (1996 est.):

Cardiff	315,040
Swansea	230,180
Newport	136,789

Famous landmarks:
- ▶ ***Beaumaris Castle***, Anglesey
- ▶ ***Conwy Castle***, Conwy
- ▶ ***Caernarfon Castle***, Caernarfon
- ▶ ***Saint David's Cathedral***, Saint David's
- ▶ ***Tintern Abbey***, Monmouthshire
- ▶ ***Big Pit Mine***, Blaenavon

Industry: Electric and electronic equipment, vehicles, chemicals, food products, metals. Agriculture: sheep, cattle, barley, wheat, potatoes. Mining: coal, iron

Currency: The British pound sterling (£) is the basic unit of currency. In August 2002, £1 equaled US$1.53.

System of weights and measures: Metric system; also some use of imperial system

Literacy rate: 99 percent

Children carry Wales's red dragon flag

Catherine Zeta-Jones

Common Welsh words and phrases:

S'mae (smy)	Hello
Hwyl (hoo-eel)	Good-bye
Sut dach chi? (sit dakh kee?)	How are you?
Iawn, diolch (ee-ow-n, dee-olkh)	Fine, thanks
Os gwelwch yn dda	Please
(oss gwe-look 'n tha)	
Diolch (dee-olkh)	Thank you
Faint? (vye-nt)	How much?

Famous Welsh People:

Sir Richard Burton *Actor*	(1925–1984)
Saint David *Christian missionary and teacher*	(520?–589)
Owen Glendower *Nationalist hero*	(1359–1416)
Sir Anthony Hopkins *Actor*	(1937–)
Tom Jones *Popular singer*	(1940–)
Richard Llewellyn *Novelist*	(1907–1983)
David Lloyd George *British prime minister*	(1863–1945)
Dylan Thomas *Poet*	(1914–1953)
Henry Tudor (Henry VII) *King of England*	(1457–1509)
Catherine Zeta-Jones *Actress*	(1969–)

To Find Out More

Nonfiction

▶ Blashfield, Jean F. *England* (Enchantment of the World, Second Series). Danbury, CT: Children's Press, 1997.

▶ Catherwood, Christopher. *Martyn Lloyd Jones: From Wales to Westminster*. Fearn, Scotland: Christian Focus Publications, 1999.

▶ Gies, Joseph and Frances. *Life in a Medieval Castle*. New York: Harper & Row, 1974.

▶ Hestler, Anna. *Wales* (Cultures of the World). Tarrytown, NY: Benchmark Books, 2001.

▶ Hinds, Kathryn. *The Celts of Northern Europe*. Tarrytown, NY: Benchmark Books, 1997.

▶ Lerner Publications Department of Geography (ed.). *Wales in Pictures*.

Minneapolis, MN: Lerner Publications, 1994.

▶ Leslie, Clare Walker and Frank E. Gerace. *The Ancient Celtic Festivals*. Rochester, VT: Inner Traditions International Ltd., 2000.

▶ Shearman, Deirdre. *David Lloyd George*. New York, NY: Chelsea House, 1988.

Fiction

▶ Bond, Nancy. *A String in the Harp*. New York: Aladdin Paperbacks, 1996.

▶ Thomas, Dylan and Fritz Eichenberg (illus.). *A Child's Christmas in Wales*. New York: New Directions, 1997.

▶ Thomas, W. Jenkyn. *The Welsh Fairy Book*. Mineola, NY: Dover Publications, 2001.

Videotapes

▶ *Discovering Wales*. 57 minutes. British Tourism Authority, 1992.

▶ *Wales: Heritage of a Nation*. Narrated by Richard Burton. 24 minutes. British Tourism Authority, 1987.

▶ *Wales: A Nationhood*. Sanctuary Digital Enterprises, 2001.

Web Sites

▶ **Spotlight on Wales**
http://www.britannia.com/celtic/wales/
A complete guide to Wales's history, culture, traditions, and sights.

▶ **BBC Wales**
http://www.bbc.co.uk/wales/about/
The British Broadcasting Corporation's Web site covering the language, history, geography, myths, and people of Wales.

▶ **Data Wales**
http://www.data-wales.co.uk/index.htm
Includes fascinating information on Wales's history and culture, including castles, Celts, and interesting historical figures.

▶ **National Assembly for Wales**
http://www.wales.gov.uk/
Provides a wealth of information on Wales's local government and economy.

▶ **The Castles of Wales**
http://www.castlewales.com/home.html
Photos, descriptions, and histories of dozens of Wales's medieval castles.

▶ **Welcome to Wales**
http://visitwales.wtb.lon.world.net
For information on historic sites, scenic locations, crafts, activities, and favorite kids' sites in Wales.

Organizations

▶ **Cymdeithas Madog**
Welsh Studies Institute in
North America, Inc.
27131 NE Miller St.
Duvall, WA 98019

▶ **National Assembly for Wales**
Public Information and
Education Office
Cardiff Bay
Cardiff CF99 1NA
Wales, United Kingdom

▶ **The Wales Office**
Office of the Secretary of State
for Wales
Gwydyr House
Whitehall
London SW1A2ER
England, United Kingdom

Index

Page numbers in *italics* indicate illustrations.

A

abbey ruins in Llangollen, 89
Aberystwyth, 22
Act of Union, 44
agriculture, 23, 68–70
Aneirin, 101
animals. *see* wildlife
Arthur, King, 39, 102–103
Augustine, Saint, 89

B

badgers, *33*, 33–34
Bardsey, 92, *92*
Bassey, Shirley, 83, 108
Battle of Bosworth, 44
Beaumaris Castle, 21, 45
Beuno, Saint, 91, 95
Big Pit Mining Museum, 67, 68, *68*
Black Mountains, 24
Blaenavon, 68
bottle-nosed dolphins, 35
boys' choir, *11*
Brecon Beacons National Park, 24
British Broadcasting Corporation
    (BBC), 77
British Railways, 76
Burton, Richard, 108

C

Cadfan, Saint, 92
Caernarfon Castle, 21, 22, 45

Calvin, John, 97
Cambrian Coast, 20, *20*
Cambrian Mountains, 18, *18*
Cardiff, 62–63
Cardiff Castle, 62, 63, 78
Cardigan Bay, 35
castles, 20, 21, 22, 42, 45, 62, 63, 78, 125
Catatonia, 110
Celtic bronze shield, *37*
Celtic crosses, *91*
chapel on Bardsey Island, *92*
Charles, Thomas, 97
Chartist riots, 48
Church of Saint Giles, 22
Church, Charlotte, 108
churches, cathedrals and abbeys, *11*, 22,
    24, 88, 89, *92*
climate, 25
coal mine, 66
communications, 77, 83
Conwy Castle, 21, 45, *45*
Cool Cymru, 110
crops, 69
cuisine, 122, 123–124
culture. *see also* religion
    Celtic pride, 79
    choirs and the Cymanfa Ganu,
        105–106
    Cool Cymru, 110
    crafts, 110
    education, 120–122
    family celebrations, 126–127

folk customs and superstitions, 111–113

food/cuisine, 122, 123–124

holidays, 121, 127, 128

influence of religion in preservation of, 47

language, 13, 48–49, 50, 61, 83–87

leeks and daffodils, 28–29

legends, myths, and tales, 19, 28, 29, 33, 38, 39, 43, 94, 102–103

literature, 107

music, 105–106

music and the arts, 108, 110–111

names/nicknames, 87

National Eisteddfod, 49, 104–105

North Wales, 82–83

poetry/poets, 95, 101–102, 103, 107

rebirth, 50–51

South Wales, 81, 82–83

sports, 63, 83, 118, 119–120

suppression by England, 48–49

traditional dress, 124–125, *125*

currency, 70, 74

customs. *see* culture; lifestyle

D

David, Saint, 29, 93–94

Deiniol, Saint, 91

devolution, 56–58

Dolbadarn Castle, 20

Druids, 32, 37–38, 99

Dylan Thomas Centre, 22

E

economy

1920s depression, 50

agriculture, 68–70

and the European Union (EU), 73–74

cost of living, 65

in the 1800s, 48

manufacturing, 71–72

tourism, 72–73

education, 120–122

Edward I, 42, 45

Edward II, 42, 45

Eisteddfod, 49, 104–105

Elizabeth II, 53, *53*

employment

agriculture, 68–70

and bilingual opportunities, 87

and the European Union (EU), 74

manufacturing, 71–72

mining, 65–68

tourism, 72–73

wages and cost of living, 65

England, union with, 44, 46

English Rule, 42–44

environmental issues, 74

European Union (EU), 73–74

Evans, Geraint, 108

F

farming, 23, 68–70

food, 122, 123–124

foot-and-mouth disease, 70, 73

forests, 27–28

G

gannets, 34, *34*

Geoffrey of Monmouth, 102–103

geography

borders/boundaries, 15–16

mountains, 18–19, 24

Northern Wales, 18–21

Southern Wales, 23–24

Gildas (monk-historian), 90, 93

Glamorgan Heritage Coast, 23–24

Glanely Gallery, 109

Glaslyn Lake, 19

Glendower, Owen, 43, *43*

Gorky's Zygotic Mynci, 110
Gorsedd of Bards, *101*, 101–102
government
    City Hall, *52*
    devolution, 56–58
    home rule, 56–58
    in the United Kingdom, 53–56
    local, 60
    National Assembly, 58–60, 74
    political parties, 60–61
Gower Peninsula, 24
gray seals, 35, *35*
Great Glasshouse, 30, *30*
Gruffudd, Ioan, 108
Gruffudd, Llywelyn ap (Llywelyn
    the Last), 42
Guildhall, 22
Gwyddfarch, Saint, 92

H

Harlech Castle, 45, *45*
Harris, Howel, 97
Hawley, Robert, *119*
Hay-on-Wye, 106, *106*
Henry V, 43
Henry VII, 44, *44*
Henry VIII, 44, 46, *46*
Hopkins, Anthony, 108, *108*
housing, 48, 115
Hywel Dda (Hywel the Good), 41

I

Illtud, Saint, 93
industry
    agriculture, 23, 68–70, 72
    manufacturing, 71–72
    mining, 23, 47–48, 49, 50, 65–68, 72
    organic farming, 69
    shipbuilding and shipping, 48
    tourism, 72–73

Island of 20,000 Saints, 92
Iwan, Dafydd, 51

J

James, Evan, 57
James, James, 57
Jones, Gwyneth, 108
Jones, Tom, 83, 108, *108*

K

Kerrigan, Justin, 111

L

labor unions, 49–50
lakes, 19
landlord system, 44, 46, 47
languages
    and Plaid Cymru, 61
    and religion, 48
    and rise in patriotism, 49
    and the National Eisteddfod, 104–105
    bilingual culture, 13, 50, 83, 86–87
    discrimination against Welsh-
        speakers, 44, 46
    English as official language, 44, 46
    North Wales, 82
    religion and Welsh, 47
    South Wales, 81
    suppression by England, 48–49
    Welsh, 83–87
    Welsh and Anglicanism, 95
    Welsh education, 122
    Welsh Language Act, 86
legends, myths, and tales, 19, 28, 29, 33,
    38, 39, 43, 94, 102–103
Lewis, Saunders, 107
lifestyle
    education, 120–122
    family celebrations, 126–127
    food/cuisine, 122, 123–124

housing, 115
  in the 1800s, 48
  leisure time, 116–117
  traditional dress, 124–125, *125*
livestock, 68–70
Llanfair Pwllgwyngyll, 87
Llanover, Lady, 124
Llechwedd Slate Caverns, 67
Llewellyn, Richard, 107
Lloyd George, David, 29, 59, *59*
Llywelyn Fawr (Llywelyn the Great),
  41–42
Llywelyn the Last, 42
Llywelyn, Gruffudd ap, 41
love spoons, 110, *110*

M
Mabinogion, 33, 103
Macdonald, Julien, 110–111
Manic Street Preachers, 110
manufacturing, 71–72
maps
  Cardiff, *63*
  geographical, *17*
  geopolitical, *12*
  Owen Glendower's revolt, *42*
  population density, *80*
  resource, *69*
  satellite view of Wales, *15*
  survival of Welsh kingdoms, *41*
  unification of Welsh kingdoms, *40*
  unitary authorities, *60*
  Welsh-speaking population, *86*
Marches/Marcher lords, 41
media, 77, 83
megaliths, 36, *36*
Melangell, Saint, 95
Merthyr riots, 48
Michael, Alun, *58*
Millennium Stadium, 63, 118, *118*
mining, 23, 38, 47–48, 49, 50, 65–68

money, 70, 74
Monmouth, 22
Monmouth Castle, 22
Monnow Bridge, 22
Morgan, Rhodri, 61, *61*
Morgan, William, 95
Morganwg, Iolo, 101
Mount Snowdon, 18–19, *19*
Museum of Welsh Life, 125
museums, 22, 23, 63, 67, 68, *68*, 109, 125
myths. *see* legends, myths and tales

N
National Botanic Garden, 30
National Eisteddfod, 49, 104–105
National Museum and Gallery, 63,
  109, *109*
national symbols
  anthem, 57
  flag, 56, *56*
  leeks and daffodils, 28–29
  red dragon, 13, *13*, 56, *56*
natural resources, 23, 38, 47–48, 49, 50,
  65–68, 72
Nennius, 102
Newport, 22
Newport Castle, 22
newspaper, 77
nicknames, 105
Norman Period, 41–42
Northern Wales, 18–21

O
Offa, 40
Offa's Dyke, *16*, 40
organic farming, 69

P
Padarn, Saint, 91
patriotism, 49

Pembrokeshire Coast, 24
people
    Celts, 37–38
    Druids, 32, 37–38, 99
    early civilizations, 37
    ethnic diversity, 80–81
    gentry, 46
    immigrants, 49
    Romans and Anglo-Saxons, 38–40
    Welsh celebrities, 107–108, *108*
    Welsh princes, 40
Plaid Cymru, 61
plant life, 27–28
    leeks and daffodils, 28–29
    National Botanic Garden, 30
polecats, 32, *32*
population
    Cardiff, 62, 80
    density, 80
    diversity, 80–81
    in the 1700s, 80
    in the 1900s, 80
    Newport, 80
    Swansea, 80
    Welsh-speaking, 86
Portmeirion, 21, *21*
Powis Castle, 21

R

radio, 77
Rebecca Riots, 48
red dragon, 13, *13*, 56, *56*
red kites, 33
red squirrel, *31*

religion
    Age of Saints, 90–95
    and Welsh language, 47
    Anglican Church, 46–47
    Anglicanism and Welsh language, 95
    Baptists, 96
    Calvinistic Methodist, 97–98
    Celtic Church, 89–90
    Christianity, 39, 89
    Church in Wales, 98
    Congregationalists, 96
    diversity in Wales, 90
    early Celtic, 38, 98–99
    holidays, 121, 127, 128
    Independents, 96
    Methodist Revival, 96–98
    missionary monks, 90–91
    Nonconformists, 96–98
    Presbyterian, 97–98
    Quakers, 96
    relics of the saints, 91
    tithes, 46–47
    United Reformed Church, 96
Rhodri Mawr (Rhodri the Great), 40
Rhys, Lord, 104, 105
Richard III, 44
riots, 48
Rolls, Charles Stewart, 22
Royal National Eisteddfod.
    see National Eisteddfod
rugby. *see* sports

S

S4C, 77

Saint David's Cathedral, *11*, 24, 93
Saint Fagan's Castle, 125
Saint Winefride's Well, 95
Saint Woolos Cathedral, 22
seabirds, 34
seal pup, *35*
Severn Bridge, *74*, 74–75
Sianel Pedwar Cymru (Channel Four Wales), 77
Skomer vole, 35
slate quarry, *47*
Snowdon Mountain Railway, 76, *76*
Snowdonia Mountain Range, 18–19
Snowdonia National Park, 20
Southern Wales, 23–24
sports, 63, 83, 118, 119–120
Statute of Rhuddlan, 42
steel-smelting plant, *71*
Stereophonics, 110, *110*
superstitions. *see* culture
Swansea, *22*, 22
Swansea Museum, 22

T

Taliesin, 101, 103
television, 77, 83
Terfel, Bryn, 108
Thomas, Dylan, 83, *100*, 107, *107*
Thomas, R.S., 107
timeline, historic, 128–129
Tintern Abbey, 88
tourism, 72–73, 75–76
trade, 48

traditions. *see* culture
transportation
    airlines, 76–77
    canals, 48
    ferries, 76
    railways, 22, 48, 75–76
    roadways, 74–75
    Transporter Bridge, 22
Treason of the Blue Books, 49
Troyes, Chrétien de, 103
Tudor, Henry. *See* Henry VII
Tysilio, Saint, 91

W

Welsh Language Act, 86
Welsh National Opera, 108
Welsh princes, 40
Welsh Rarebit (recipe), 122
Wesley, John, 97
wildlife
    badgers, *33*, 33–34
    coastal, 33–34
    in forests and valleys, 31–33
    long-horned white cattle, 32, *32*
    protection, 27
William the Conqueror, 41
Williams, Peter, 85
Williams-Ellis, Clough, 21
Winefride, Saint, 95
Wrexham, 22

Z

Zeta-Jones, Catherine, 108, *108*

Meet the Author

ANN HEINRICHS fell in love with faraway places while reading Doctor Dolittle books as a child. Now she tries to cover as much of the world as possible. She has traveled through most of the United States and much of Europe, as well as the Middle East, East Asia, and Africa. In Wales she enjoyed trekking through the countryside, scrambling up rocky hillsides, and exploring medieval castles, cathedrals, and ancient sites. Because her maternal grandfather's family was Welsh, she felt a certain sense of homecoming there.

Ann grew up roaming the woods of Arkansas. Now she lives in Chicago. She is the author of more than eighty books for children and young adults on American, European, Asian, and African history and culture. Several of her books have won national awards.

"To me, writing nonfiction is a bigger challenge than writing fiction. With nonfiction, you can't just dream something up—everything has to be true. Finding facts is harder than

making things up, but to me it's more rewarding. When I uncover the facts, they always turn out to be more spectacular than fiction could ever be. And I'm always on the lookout for what kids in another country are up to, so I can report back to kids here."

Ann has also written numerous newspaper, magazine, and encyclopedia articles. As an advertising copywriter, she has covered everything from plumbing hardware to Oriental rugs. She holds bachelor's and master's degrees in piano performance. But these days her performing arts are t'ai chi empty-hand and sword forms. She is an award-winning martial artist and participates in regional and national tournaments.

Photo Credits

A Perfect Exposure: 22, 100, 130 left (Liz Barry), 89 (Bob Jones)

Anthony Pugliese: 143

AP/Wide World Photos: 58 (Barry Batchelor), 119 (John Cogill), 118 (Max Nash)

Bridgeman Art Library International Ltd., London/New York: 102 (Biblioteca Nazionale, Turin, Italy/Roget-Viollet, Paris), 101 (The Royal Cornwall Museum, Truro, Cornwall, UK)

Britain on View/British Tourist Authority/www.britainonview.com: 9 (Barry Hick), 104,109

Churchill & Klehr Photography: 43, 85, 116, 123

Corbis Images: 125 bottom (Dave Bartruff), 51 (Hans Bauman/ Hulton-Deutsch Collection), 44, 99 (Bettmann), 78 (Jan Butchofsky-Houser), 32 bottom (Robert Dowling), 16 (Robert Estall), 11 (Macduff Everton), 92 (Alison Hall/Cordaiy Photo Library Ltd.), 20, 67, 106 (Dave G. Houser), 47, 54, 59 (Hulton-Deutsch Collection), 19 (John Noble), 2 (Richard T. Nowitz), 8 (Philip Panton/Eye Ubiquitous), 82 (Adam Woolfitt)

Crefftau Aberarth Crafts/Marian and Roy Phillips: 110 bottom

FPG International/Getty Images/ Telegraph Colour Library: 74

Getty Images: 108 top left (Richard Kille/In Focus), 13, 61 110 top, 133 top (Simon Ridgway)

Greg Gawlowski: 81 bottom, 88

H. Armstrong Roberts, Inc./George Hunter: 21, 45 bottom

Hulton | Archive/Getty Images: 108 top right, 133 bottom (Munawar Hosain/ Fotos International)

ImageState/Chris Warren: 76

National Museums and Galleries of Wales: 111 (Frederic Evans), 112 (Tony Hadland)

North Wind Picture Archives: 38

Peter Arnold Inc.: 14, 18, 131 bottom (J. Baxter/Woodfall Wild Images), 7 bottom, 73, 114, 117 (David Woodfall/Woodfall Wild Images)

Photo Researchers, NY: 79 (Spencer Grant), 36, 66 (Farrell Grehan), 15 (M-SAT LTD/SPL), 124 (Richard T. Nowitz), 32 top (Roger Wilmshurst)

Photofest: 107 (Rollie Mckenna), 108 bottom

Scotland in Focus: 31, 35 (P. Cairns), 29, 34 (L. Campbell), 27 (M. Moar)

Stock Montage, Inc.: 39, 46

Stone/Getty Images: 33 (Laurie Campbell), 23 (Paul Harris), 24 (Nigel Hillier), cover, 6 (John Lawrence), 71 (James Nelson), 28 (Andy Sacks), 52 (Stephen Studd), 115 (Trevor Wood), 26 (David Woodfall)

Superstock, Inc.: 45 top, 62, 70, 132 top, 132 bottom

The Image Works: 64 (Suzanne Arms), 68 top, 83 (Stuart Cohen), 93 (Macduff Everton), 53, 125 top (Topham)

The Photolibrary Wales: 81 top, 91, 94, 121, 122, 126, 127

Tim Thompson: 30, 75

Woodfin Camp & Associates: 25, 68 bottom (Timothy Eagan)

Maps by Joe LeMonnier